Voting Behavior:
The 2000 Election

Charles Prysby
University of North Carolina at Greensboro

Carmine Scavo
East Carolina University

Distributed by the
American Political Science Association
and the
Inter-University Consortium for
Political and Social Research

Acknowledgments

We are grateful to the American Political Science Association (APSA) and the Inter-University Consortium for Political and Social Research (ICPSR) for their support. The APSA and the ICPSR have supported the SETUPS series since 1974, when the first SETUPS were created. We are pleased that they have continued this activity, and we are especially grateful to Sheilah Mann, APSA Director of Education and Professional Development, for her continuing role in supporting this project. Michelle Prysby read the entire manuscript, and her suggested changes improved the final product. Sandy Maisel also reviewed the materials and made useful suggestions. The authors, of course, bear full responsibility for the contents of this book and the accompanying dataset.

Preface

Voting Behavior: The 2000 Election is a new SETUPS (*Supplemental Empirical Teaching Units in Political Science*) that offers an accessible dataset drawn from the American National Election Study of the 2000 presidential election. Charles Prysby and Carmine Scavo—authors of SETUPS on the 1984, 1988, 1992, and 1996 presidential elections and the SETUPS that examines American voting behavior over twenty years—developed this new SETUPS to give faculty and students access to the major scholarly survey of attitudes, attributes, and vote choice in the 2000 national election. The Inter-University Consortium for Political and Social Research (ICPSR) at the University of Michigan has collaborated with APSA since 1974 to develop and sustain the distribution of SETUPS. ICPSR will distribute the 2000 SETUPS dataset in a somewhat different manner than it distributed earlier versions. The files for SETUPS 2000 are available to ICPSR members either through direct downloading from the ICPSR website (www.icpsr.umich.edu) or through their local ICPSR Official Representative. Faculty at non-ICPSR member colleges and universities will receive a data order form with their shipments of SETUPS manuals from APSA. Once the data order form is submitted to ICPSR, the SETUPS 2000 files will be supplied on CD-ROM. Included on the CD-ROM will be data and documentation files along with SAS, SPSS, and STATA data definition statements for use with each of those popular statistical analysis software packages.

The SETUPS in this series are designed for use in courses on American government and politics. The SETUPS in American Politics Series was introduced in 1974, and it is used in colleges and universities throughout the United States and abroad.

Other SETUPS in American Politics currently available through APSA:

Voting Behavior: The 1996 Election
    by Charles Prysby and Carmine Scavo
American Voting Behavior in Presidential Elections from 1972 to 1992
    by Charles Prysby and Carmine Scavo
Voting Behavior: The 1992 Election
    by Charles Prysby and Carmine Scavo

See page 113 for information on ordering these publications.

Cover illustration by Ray Driver and cover design by Rich Pottern. Project direction by Sheilah Mann, APSA Director of Education and Professional Development. Final copyediting, layout and production management by Polly Karpowicz. Printed by Fontana Lithograph.

ISBN: 1-878147-35-8

Table of Contents

Chapter I
The 2000 Presidential Election

Some presidential elections lack drama and suspense. One candidate emerges as the leader soon after the nominations and remains ahead throughout the campaign. Campaign events seem to have little influence on voter preferences. The election outcome comes as no surprise. The front runner wins a clear victory on election day. The loser, who appears in retrospect to have had little real chance of winning, quickly concedes. The election is effectively over immediately after election day, even though the electoral college will not officially cast its votes for several weeks. Attention is quickly turned to the incoming administration. Many presidential elections display this pattern, but 2000 was not such a year.

The 2000 presidential election confounded many experts. A number of political scientists, relying on models that had accurately predicted most recent presidential election outcomes, made early, pre-campaign predictions that Al Gore would win a significant majority of the popular vote (Campbell 2001). Many pollsters, using public opinion data collected in late October, projected a narrow but clear majority of the vote for George W. Bush (Voter.com 2000). Near the end, some analysts thought that Gore might win the electoral college vote while losing the popular vote (Erickson and Sigman 2000). All these predictions were wrong.

The outcome was the closest presidential election in modern times. As the title of one book stated, it was "the perfect tie" (Ceasar and Busch 2001). Both the popular vote and the electoral college vote were almost evenly divided. Adding to the drama and suspense was the fact that the outcome was not known on the day following the election. Uncertainty over the true vote totals in Florida made it impossible to determine immediately who would finally win that state's electoral college votes. Without Florida, neither candidate had a majority of the electors. Weeks passed while attorneys for the two campaigns pursued a variety of legal actions aimed at requiring or at stopping vote recounts. Bush finally won Florida, but only after a controversial Supreme Court decision in December, over a month after election day. To use a sports analogy, it was as if the Super Bowl outcome had been decided by one point in the final seconds on a controversial play. Moreover, while Bush ultimately won a narrow majority of the electoral college vote, he trailed Gore slightly in the popular vote, making him the only president elected in the twentieth century without a plurality of the popular vote.

Background to the 2000 Presidential Election

What happened in 2000 was influenced by the events of the previous eight years. The accomplishments, scandals, and conflicts surrounding the Clinton administration set the stage for the subsequent presidential election. In the last year of his administration, President Clinton had fairly strong public job approval ratings. An October Gallup poll showed a 58% job approval rating for the outgoing president, which was similar to what polls that spring and summer had found (Gallup Organization 2000a). Democrats were encouraged by the fact that a clear majority of Americans approved of Clinton's performance as president. Any incumbent vice-president running to become president is helped greatly by a favorable rating of the outgoing president. Indeed, George W. Bush's father, George H. W. Bush, was elected president in just such a situation in 1988, when he succeeded Ronald Reagan as president. Vice President Gore simply hoped to repeat the 1988 outcome.

Clinton's favorable approval ratings rested largely on the fact that the country enjoyed peace and prosperity. In particular, the economy performed extremely well during his two terms in office. Clinton defeated George H. W. Bush in the 1992 presidential election in large part because of feelings that Bush had mismanaged the economy. Under Clinton, the country enjoyed eight years of economic growth with low inflation. Partly because of the good economy and partly because of the tax and spending policies supported by Clinton and the Congress, the enormous budget deficits that existed in the late 1980s and early 1990s were turned into budget surpluses by 2000. Almost no one in 1992 would have predicted such a rosy eight years of prosperity. In short, it was an economic record that any vice president who was running for president would love to defend.

However, the favorable public opinion of Clinton's performance as president was not matched by similarly high evaluations of him as a person. From the very beginning, scandals plagued Clinton. In 1992, before he had even been nominated, charges of extra-marital affairs surfaced. Accusations of wrong-doing on the part of Clinton regarding a real estate project while he was governor of Arkansas, the so-called "Whitewater" affair, resulted in the appointment of an independent counsel to investigate the matter after Clinton was elected president. Other accusations of ethical or legal violations arose throughout the Clinton administration, including charges that he and Vice President Gore inappropriately used their offices to raise campaign funds.

In early 1998, the Monica Lewinski scandal began and subsequently produced the most controversy and conflict. Evidence emerged that President Clinton had an affair with Lewinski, a White House intern, and that he lied about the affair in a recent deposition, taken because of a civil suit filed by a former Arkansas state employee, Paula Jones, who alleged that Clinton sexually harassed her when he was governor. The independent counsel who had been handling the Whitewater investigation, Kenneth Starr, became involved in the investigation of the charges regarding the Lewinski matter from the very beginning. Clinton initially denied that the allegations were true, but Starr vigorously pursued the investigation through the spring and summer of 1998. In August, Starr finally forced Clinton to provide testimony to a federal grand jury, at which point Clinton admitted having an inappropriate relationship with Lewinski, although he argued that the testimony that he provided in his earlier deposition was legally accurate, given his understanding of the legal definition of sexual relations. Starr, however, concluded in a report released the following month that Clinton had committed perjury and obstruction of justice. Starr's report outlined eleven possible grounds for impeachment.

Republicans, who controlled both houses of Congress, pushed for the impeachment of Clinton, arguing that by falsely testifying in his deposition and by attempting to cover up the truth, he had failed to uphold his oath of office to "faithfully execute the laws." Most Democrats argued that Clinton's behavior, while personally reprehensible, did not rise to the level of an impeachable offense. Public opinion polls showed that the majority of Americans agreed with this view

(Gallup Organization 1998). Still, the Republican leaders in the House forged ahead, and in October, 1998, the House of Representatives voted to launch an impeachment inquiry. The vote in the House was largely along party lines. In December, the House Judiciary Committee voted for articles of impeachment, largely along party lines, and shortly afterward the full House voted to impeach the president, again largely along party lines. President Clinton became only the second president in history to be impeached (The first, President Andrew Johnson, was impeached, but not convicted, in 1865).

In the subsequent trial in the Senate, a two-thirds vote was necessary to convict the president. Even if all Republicans supported conviction, a number of Democratic votes would still be needed, which seemed less and less likely as the trial progressed. When the Senate voted on the two articles of impeachment in February, a number of Republican senators joined every Democratic senator to vote both articles down. Neither article received more than 50 of the 100 votes. Clinton remained in office, and a March, 1999, Gallup poll showed that he had a 64% job approval rating, higher than what it had been in January, 1998, when the scandal first surfaced (Gallup Organization 1999).

The Lewinski and other scandals associated with President Clinton affected both presidential candidates in 2000. Al Gore did not want voters to link him with their concerns over Clinton's moral and ethical behavior. At the same time, Gore wanted to take credit for the economic and other accomplishments of the Clinton years. Distancing himself from all of the controversy surrounding Clinton while still associating himself with the economic accomplishments of the administration proved to be a difficult task for Gore. His campaign for president may have suffered because of that conflict. In particular, he did not want Clinton to campaign heavily for him, even though the president was popular among many Democratic groups and might have helped in some key states.

The Republican presidential candidate, George W. Bush, naturally hoped that disapproval of Clinton's personal behavior would help the Republican cause. Yet he had concerns about how the public reacted to the impeachment of Clinton. Many Americans seemed to feel that the Republicans in Congress had gone too far and that the Republican congressional leaders were too extreme. As mentioned above, Clinton's job approval rating following the failed attempt to remove him from office was slightly higher than what it was before the Lewinski stories first appeared in the media. The best explanation for this surprising result is not that the American public approved of Clinton's behavior but that they disapproved of the actions of congressional Republicans (and perhaps of the media's intense and detailed coverage of the scandal). Perceptions of the congressional Republicans as too extreme contributed to the poor showing that Republican congressional candidates made in the 1998 elections, a point that was not lost on Bush.

Moreover, feeling that the congressional Republicans were too extreme predated the impeachment debate. After the Republicans took control of both houses of Congress in the 1994 mid-term elections, they hoped to make a number of significant changes in public policy. Indeed, most House of Representatives Republican candidates campaigned in 1994 on just such a pledge, the "Contract with America." Headed by Newt Gingrich, who became the Republican Speaker of the House following the 1994 election, Republicans seemed uninterested in compromising with President Clinton, whom they regarded as repudiated by the 1994 election results.

The key conflicts in 1995 centered around the budget. Clinton opposed the Republican budget proposals, and the conflict between the legislative and executive branches resulted in the government having to shut down twice, for a total of four weeks. Congressional Republicans believed that the public would blame the president for the shutdown, but the public felt otherwise. President Clinton's approval rating rose to over 50% in late 1995, while Gingrich became one of the least approved elected federal officials (Gallup Organization 1996).

Conflicts between President Clinton and congressional Republicans influenced Bush's campaign strategy. Bush did not want to defend the Republican impeachment effort, nor did he want to be too closely identified with some of the more conservative members of the Republican congressional leadership. At the same time, he wanted to exploit the possible advantage that he might obtain from the Clinton scandals. He attempted to accomplish this goal in part by emphasizing that he was not a part of the Washington elite but a governor who, he claimed, had been able to bring Republicans and Democrats in the Texas legislature together to accomplish goals. Also, he called himself a "compassionate conservative," thereby suggesting that he was more moderate than some in his party. Bush also spoke in general terms about restoring honor and dignity to the White House, a subtle way of drawing attention to the Clinton scandals.

Nominations

Both Gore and Bush began the primary season as the front runners in their respective parties. Both secured their nomination before the end of March. The relatively early conclusions to the nomination battles in both parties was in part a reflection of the fact that the caucuses and primaries in 2000 were heavily front-loaded. This tendency for states to move up their primary or caucus dates, in order to be more influential in the nominating process, had been occurring since the reforms of the early 1970s established the presidential primaries as the dominant method of selection of convention delegates. In 2000, two-thirds of the delegates in each party were selected in primaries or caucuses held before the middle of March. By comparison, fewer that one-half of the delegates were selected that early in 1984 (Mayer 2001, 14).

The very early contests, such as the Iowa caucuses and the New Hampshire primary, were particularly important. Even though these were small states, with relatively few delegates to the nominating conventions, the media coverage of these events would be great. Winning either or both contests would provide a candidate with large amounts of favorable media exposure, which would most likely help the candidate to do better in subsequent primaries or caucuses. Failing to win a single early contest most likely would effectively extinguish the hopes of most candidates.

The Democratic Nomination

It was not surprising that Gore was the early front runner among Democrats. Incumbent vice presidents are usually leading candidates for the presidential nomination when the incumbent president is not running for reelection. In the previous three times where this was the situation–1960, 1968, and 1988–the vice president received his party's nomination. Serving as vice president, especially in modern times, provides an individual with considerable resources. Among other things, the vice president is able to build support among party leaders around the country, to raise substantial campaign funds, and to spend a great deal of time campaigning. Moreover, Gore was an extremely active vice president, one who played a visible role in the Clinton administration. When the vice president has the support of his president, which Gore had, his advantage is very substantial. There were some concerns among Democrats that Gore was not a very dynamic candidate, but his support among core Democratic groups was solid.

Gore's position discouraged most other potential candidates from even challenging him for the nomination. While several potential candidates considered running against Gore, only one Democrat, former U.S. senator Bill Bradley, decided to enter the primaries. A former Rhodes scholar and professional basketball player, Bradley served for three terms as the senator from New Jersey. He left the Senate in 1996, stating that he wanted to devote time to other endeavors. While a senator, he was widely regarded as thoughtful and knowledgeable. He also had a good reputation for personal integrity. He was not, however, thought of as highly charismatic or as a great campaigner. Some even considered him dull. Nevertheless, Bradley at one point appeared to be seriously challenging Gore. Most importantly, Bradley was able to raise substantial campaign funds. In fact, in January, 2000, he and Gore were roughly equal in the campaign funds that they had raised, around $30 million each (Corrado 2001, 104). Also, the Gore campaign suffered from organizational problems in 1999, and Gore himself struggled to project a consistent image.

As the first nomination contests approached, Gore focused sharp attacks on several of Bradley's policy positions. The aggressive Gore campaign appeared to work. Bradley seemed unwilling or unprepared to respond to the attacks, preferring to run a more positive campaign. Gore won the Iowa caucuses, the first official nomination contests, by a substantial margin. This outcome made the next event, the New Hampshire primary, crucial for Bradley. A victory here was almost essential to provide his campaign with some impetus. Unfortunately for Bradley, he lost New Hampshire as well. Gore's victory in New Hampshire was a narrow one, but it was a victory, and it provided him with favorable media coverage. In contrast, Bradley found it difficult to attract substantial media coverage after New Hampshire. Gore won the remaining primary contests by wide margins, rarely receiving less than 60% of the vote (Stanley 2001, 40). By mid-March, Gore had effectively won the nomination. Moreover, the nomination contest had not seriously divided the party. Some analysts felt that Gore even benefitted from the Bradley challenge, although there was some public perception that Gore was too aggressive in his attacks on Bradley.

The Republican Nomination

Bush had a somewhat more difficult challenge to overcome. First, there were many Republican candidates for the nomination. Some, such as Alan Keyes or Gary Bauer, were clearly extremely long shots for the nomination. Others, however, appeared on paper to be stronger contenders. Bush's better-known challengers included former vice president Dan Quayle, Senators John McCain and Orrin Hatch, former cabinet secretary Elizabeth Dole, publisher and previous presidential candidate Steve Forbes, and former Tennessee governor Lamar Alexander.

Bush was the front runner in this crowded field from the beginning, even though his political experience (apart from being the son of a former president) was limited to serving as governor of Texas. One reason for Bush's leading position was his ability to raise enormous sums of campaign money. By January, 2000, he had raised 60 million dollars, far more than any other presidential candidate had ever raised for the nomination (Corrado 2001, 100). Bush raised so much money that he chose not to accept federal matching funds for his campaign. By forgoing matching funds, Bush was not bound by any spending limitations, which were a requirement for accepting such funds. In particular, by avoiding spending limitations, Bush would be able to significantly outspend his opposition in the small early states, such as Iowa and New Hampshire.

Bush's status as the front runner was not solely a function of his ability to raise campaign funds. As governor of Texas, he was reelected by a landslide in 1998. His ability to win votes from normally Democratic groups in Texas, including Hispanics, led many Republicans to believe that he would appeal well to swing voters, whose support was crucial for winning a presidential election. At the same time, he was clearly acceptable to most solidly Republican groups, such as Christian conservatives. Many Republican party leaders coalesced behind Bush relatively early, partly because they saw the other Republican candidates as lacking a broad appeal. These party leaders also saw Bush as a good candidate because, as discussed earlier, he was a governor and therefore not part of the Washington elite. Bush received the endorsement of most of his fellow Republican governors, as well as the endorsement of many Republican members of Congress (Ceasar and Bush 2001, 68).

There were some concerns about Bush as a presidential candidate. He had limited political experience, and he seemed not particularly knowledgeable about world affairs. He also had deficiencies as a public speaker, including a tendency to make verbal gaffes. Some analysts wondered if, as a presidential candidate, Bush would hold his own in debates. There also were vague charges, never substantiated, that he had used cocaine earlier in his life. Bush refused to confirm or deny these or other rumors about his behavior as a younger adult, other than to admit that he at one time drank too much, which led him to refrain completely from consuming alcohol. This admission did not seem to greatly concern voters.

Senator McCain presented the strongest challenge to Bush. McCain lacked the financial resources of Bush, but he had some appealing personal attributes. He was a war hero, a navy aviator who had been shot down and held as a prisoner of war in Vietnam for several years. He also had a reputation for being an independent--some would even say a maverick--Republican. McCain, who made campaign finance reform one of his key issues, was seen by some as the kind of Republican who would easily win over independent and moderate voters. Unfortunately for McCain, he did not appeal as well to conservative Republicans, who were far more numerous among voters in Republican presidential primaries. Furthermore, he had difficulty in obtaining endorsements from Republican leaders and elected officials. Even among his fellow U.S. senators, McCain obtained far fewer endorsements than did Bush (Ceasar and Busch 2001, 68).

Bush won the first nomination event, the Iowa caucuses, by a wide margin, putting his campaign off to a good start. One week later, his nomination campaign ran into a roadblock. McCain, who decided not to compete in Iowa, won the New

Hampshire primary by a decisive margin, contrary to the expectations of many political observers (Crotty 2001, 102). The victory gave him much needed media exposure. Bush responded to this defeat by campaigning harder for the votes of conservative Republicans, who played a bigger role in many other primaries than they did in New Hampshire. McCain had difficulty in following up his New Hampshire success with additional victories. In the four weeks following the New Hampshire primary, McCain won only the Arizona and Michigan primaries, the former of which was his home state, while Bush won primaries in South Carolina, Delaware, Virginia, and Washington (Mayer 2001, 34-37). On March 7, termed "Super Tuesday," twelve states held primaries. Bush won nine states, including all the large ones. McCain won only three smaller states in New England (Stanley 2001, 43-44). At this point, Bush had a commanding lead in delegates and in financial resources. McCain ceased to be a serious challenger, and he withdrew his candidacy at this time.

Like Gore, Bush effectively secured the nomination months before the convention, with a united party behind him, although McCain, while he endorsed Bush as the Republican nominee, never seemed enthusiastic in his support. However, in appealing to conservative forces in the party to win the nomination, Bush failed to develop the image of a more moderate Republican that he had hoped to project. Still, public opinion polls showed Bush to be running slightly ahead of Gore at this time (Gallup Organization 2000c).

The Campaign

After capturing their nominations in March, both Bush and Gore turned their attention to the general election campaign. With over seven months until the November election, both candidates had considerable time to develop their image and appeal. Both candidates had weak points that they hoped to strengthen and themes that they wished to emphasize, and their campaign strategies and tactics reflected those concerns. Voters received information about the candidates through a variety of sources and formats. Some of this information, such as campaign speeches or televised campaign commercials, could be carefully controlled by the two campaigns; other information, such as reporting in the print and broadcast media, could only indirectly be influenced by the candidates. With polls showing the two candidates fairly close, the general election campaign was crucial.

Bush began his campaign for the nomination portraying himself as a moderate Republican, but the fight with McCain for the nomination forced Bush to emphasize his conservative credentials. With the nomination contest over, Bush again attempted to define himself as a moderate conservative. In general terms, he referred to himself as a "compassionate conservative" and talked about his ability as governor to bring Democrats and Republicans together in Texas. He also spoke repeatedly about his support for government spending on education and health care. On education, he proposed increased federal government spending, coupled with increased requirements for testing by the schools. In the health area, he proposed a federal government prescription drug plan addition to Medicare. Neither of these positions were ones normally associated with conservative Republicans.

The Republican nominating convention reinforced the moderate and inclusive nature of Bush's campaign message. The party appeared highly unified behind

Bush. Divisive issues were played down. Most of the highly conservative Republican members of Congress stayed in the background. Minority speakers were particularly visible to the television audience. In part, the Bush strategists were able to spotlight the moderate side of the candidate because Bush's standing among conservative groups was secure. The convention seemed to be a very successful campaign event. Public opinion polls taken a few days after the conclusion of the convention showed Bush leading Gore by over seventeen percentage points (Gallup Organization 2000c).

In many ways, Gore also could claim to be a moderate within his own party. While in Congress, he was a member of the Democratic Leadership Council, a group of moderate Democrats. He was one of the Democratic senators who joined with Republicans to support U.S. military action against Iraq in the 1991 Gulf War. As a candidate for the presidential nomination in 1988, he presented himself as a moderate southern Democrat who would be capable of carrying southern states in the general election, unlike some of the liberal Democratic candidates. As vice president, he was associated with the policies of the Clinton administration, which pursued more moderate policies after the Republicans took control of Congress in 1994. Large, new government programs, such as the national health care system proposed by Clinton during his first administration, were absent from the second administration. These more centrist policies, along with the budget surpluses that were now being generated, supported the view that Gore was a moderate Democrat.

However, Gore attempted to paint himself as a populist on a number of issues. He spoke generally about his willingness to fight for the people against powerful special interests. He claimed that he was the candidate who would fight for the patient against the health insurance industry and against the pharmaceutical industry. He said that he, not Bush, would protect the environment against potential polluters, such as the oil industry. Moreover, his past environmental proposals, including an earlier book on this topic, reinforced an image of a candidate who emphasized environmental protection. These populist pronouncements contrasted with the more moderate aspects of Gore's image, making any ideological placement of him difficult.

Although Bush and Gore were generally considered not to be extremists within their respective parties, they differed on almost every major policy issue. In many cases the differences were a matter of degree or of details, and perhaps some of the distinctions were not clear to less informed voters, but the differences were there. On all major policy dimensions—taxation, economic and social welfare issues, social issues, and foreign affairs and defense issues—the two candidates differed along basic liberal-conservative lines.

Taxation was an important issue in the campaign (Clymer 2000). Bush championed a broad tax cut, arguing that the budget surpluses were the "people's money" and that they deserved to have it back. Gore also favored a tax cut, but one that was smaller and more targeted and one that was less favorable to upper income groups. Gore criticized the Bush tax plan as one that was heavily slanted toward the wealthiest Americans and that would endanger the years of economic prosperity and the budget surpluses that materialized during the Clinton administration. Bush criticized the Gore plan as beneficial only to some taxpayers, whereas he claimed that his plan gave all taxpayers relief.

Spending on education and social welfare programs also received considerable attention in the campaign. Both candidates favored increased federal government spending on education, but their plans differed. The most notable difference was over publically funded vouchers that parents could in some circumstances use to send their children to private schools, a proposal that Bush favored and Gore opposed (Balz and Morin 2000). Another case of subtle differences between the policy proposals of the two candidates involved plans to add prescription drug coverage to Medicare. Gore's plan was more extensive than the one put forth by Bush, but the differences in the details of the two plans may have been lost to many voters (Toner 2000b). Differences on social security were more pronounced (Mitchell 2000). Bush proposed a partial privatization of social security, which he claimed was necessary to save the system. Gore flatly opposed privatization and offered his own plan for social security reform.

Environmental issues clearly differentiated the candidates (Barstow 2000; Toner 2000a). Bush favored more exploration for oil and gas deposits, even in environmentally sensitive areas, such as the Arctic National Wildlife Refuge. Gore argued against permitting drilling in the ANWR and other currently protected areas. Bush also opposed the Kyoto treaty, which would commit the United States and other countries to substantially reducing their production of greenhouse gases, which come largely from the burning of fossil fuels. Gore not only supported the treaty but had played a critical role in negotiating it. Bush's environmental record while governor of Texas became an issue during the campaign, as Gore criticized Bush for being a governor who was far too friendly toward polluters.

A number of social and moral issues revealed clear differences between the two candidates. On abortion, Gore took a strong pro-choice stance, while Bush was solidly pro-life. Bush opposed increased gun control efforts, which Gore generally defended, although he sometimes qualified his support. Bush called for funneling federal money for social programs through faith-based groups, something that raised questions about the separation of church and state.

Foreign policy and defense issues occupied less attention in the campaign, perhaps because there were no foreign crises or major problems facing the country at the time. Still, the candidates differed in this area as well. Bush called for higher levels of defense spending than did Gore, for example. However, the more important question in this area was not where the two candidates stood on specific issues, but on whether Bush had sufficient knowledge of foreign policy to be president. Lacking in Washington experience, not having other involvement in foreign affairs, and sometimes responding with weak answers to questions from reporters in this area, Bush strove during the campaign to demonstrate that he was capable of being the nation's commander-in-chief.

In sum, Bush and Gore differed along basic liberal-conservative lines. Compared to Bush, Gore favored more spending on programs aimed at helping the economically disadvantaged, less spending on defense, a tax system that would place more of the burden on wealthier individuals, more environmental regulation, and more liberal policies on social issues, such as abortion. But while the candidates differed on a wide range of issues, it is not clear that either candidate had a significant advantage on policy issues. Bush was somewhat to the right of the median voter, while Gore was somewhat to the left. If one candidate attracted more voters because of his issue positions, it probably was by only a small margin—although given the closeness of the election, even a small number of additional votes might have been decisive.

The campaign was not just about policy issues. Both candidates devoted considerable attention to developing their personal image. In each case, the candidate had concerns that he hoped could be ameliorated during the campaign. As mentioned above, one of the greatest concerns of Bush and his strategists was that the voters might see the Republican nominee as insufficiently knowledgeable about government matters, particularly foreign affairs. Both Bush's lack of government experience and his tendency to make verbal misstatements contributed to these perceptions. The concerns over these perceptions were an important reason why Bush selected Richard Cheney, a former member of Congress and secretary of defense in the administration of George H. W. Bush, as his running mate. Cheney's lengthy experience in Washington helped to counterbalance Bush's limited government experience. Concerns over Bush's competence also made his convention acceptance speech and his debates with Gore particularly important. Poor performances in these widely viewed events would have devastated his chances for election. Fortunately for Bush, he did reasonably well in these events, undoubtedly far exceeding the expectations of many.

Bush also attempted to exploit what he thought was the biggest shortcoming of the Clinton administration, the numerous scandals discussed earlier, by emphasizing that he would restore honor and dignity to the White House. Thus, character became an important component of the Bush campaign message. As a positive message, Bush spoke in general terms about his character and integrity. As a negative message, Bush assailed Gore's integrity.

Gore was also concerned about public perception of his personal character. While most voters saw him as experienced and knowledgeable, he was not so widely perceived as warm or inspiring. Throughout his eight years as vice president, Gore was thought of as somewhat aloof, cool, and even stiff. Indeed, Gore often joked about this characterization at his own expense, which clearly was an attempt to project a warmer image. Still, such an image was not easily reshaped, and Gore probably suffered on this dimension from a comparison to Bush, who came across as more likeable to many voters. During the first presidential debate, for example, Gore repeatedly showed visible exasperation with Bush's remarks and often replied in a condescending manner, to the point that some viewers felt annoyed by Gore's behavior (Nelson 2001, 77). In the subsequent debates, Gore carefully avoided such behavior.

Gore also had to contend with perceptions that he was not always honest–that he would stretch the truth or modify his positions just to win votes. Just as the media focused on questions about Bush's competence and experience, they focused on questions of Gore's truthfulness. For example, in one of the debates, Gore used an example of medical charges paid by his mother-in-law, but it was subsequently revealed that the figures instead were drawn from a report. The Bush campaign naturally drew attention to questions about Gore's honesty. For example, Republicans mocked Gore for earlier claiming that he had invented the Internet, a statement that had received considerable play in the press (although the truth was that Gore claimed that while in the Senate he played a key role in enacting legislation that fostered the growth of the Internet, a claim that was correct). The Bush campaign also questioned the truthfulness of Gore's claim that he was unaware that a 1996 rally that he attended at a California Buddhist temple was a fund-raising event, an incident that received considerable media attention as an example of questionable fund-raising practices by the Clinton administration.

Unlike most recent presidential campaigns, the candidates in 2000 did not focus very much on the performance of the incumbent administration. In 1996, for example, President Clinton made the prosperity of his first four years the central theme in his reelection campaign. In 1992, candidate Clinton repeatedly attacked the administration of George H. W. Bush for its economic failures. As mentioned earlier, the eight years of peace and prosperity seemed at first to be a natural thing for Gore to emphasize over and over--and, of course, something for Bush to downplay. Moreover, the eight years of prosperity under the Democratic administration could be contrasted with the economic problems of the previous Republican administration, the administration of George H. W. Bush, presumably something that Gore would want to do. But the unusual circumstances of the Clinton administration led Gore to question whether he should base his campaign on the accomplishments of the Clinton administration. Gore and his strategists feared that a strong emphasis on the accomplishments of the Clinton administration would run a risk of activating "Clinton fatigue," a term that referred to general voter weariness with the personal shortcomings of the incumbent president.

Gore resolved this dilemma by distancing himself from Clinton. He chose not to base his campaign message on the accomplishments of the Clinton administration, although he did refer to them throughout his campaign. Instead, Gore talked more about his positions on various policy issues, frequently emphasizing how he would fight to protect the people. For vice president, he selected Connecticut senator Joseph Lieberman, who had been publically critical of Clinton's behavior during the Lewinski scandal. Many observers felt that Lieberman was selected by Gore in part because he felt that Lieberman's criticism of Clinton would help to separate the Gore-Lieberman ticket from the scandals of the Clinton administration. As part of this strategy to distance himself from Clinton, Gore kept Clinton from campaigning heavily for the Democratic ticket. Since Clinton remained popular among core Democratic groups, this was a controversial campaign decision.

Viewing the campaign in retrospect helps us to see why the election was so close. Neither candidate had a substantial advantage on issues, even thought they differed on most policy questions. Both had personal liabilities, although of vastly different sorts. The peace and prosperity of the Clinton administration was not a big advantage for Gore, as he chose not to emphasize it. Both candidates were quite acceptable to their core groups. Liberal Democrats had many reasons to vote for Gore. Conservative Republicans had just as many reasons to vote for Bush. Independent and swing voters, who held the balance of electoral power, were pulled in both directions by a variety of factors.

The closeness of the election was matched by volatility in the standing of the candidates. Bush was slightly ahead in March, when both candidates effectively won their nominations. During the spring and summer, Bush moved further ahead. Before the conventions began in August, Bush led Gore by about 10 points (Gallup Organization 2000c). Both candidates received a post convention bounce, but Gore's was larger. By Labor Day, Gore was ahead by about 5 points, and he remained ahead during September (Gallup Organization 2000b). During October, when the three debates were held, Bush moved ahead again (Frankovic and McDermott). A week before the election, Bush had a narrow but significant lead.

During the final week, Gore narrowed the gap. Based on results of the final polls taken just before election day, most analysts said that the race was too close to call (Elder 2000).

The fact that Bush moved ahead during October is striking. Many observers felt that the debates would allow Gore to widen his lead over Bush. Gore was seen as a skilled debater. He performed well in his vice presidential debates in 1992 and 1996, and he also did very well in a widely watched debate with Ross Perot in 1993 over the North American Free Trade Agreement. Bush, on the other hand had limited debate experience. He did participate in some debates for the Republican nomination, but most of them featured a number of candidates, so less attention was focused on any one individual. Moreover, Bush's propensity to make mis-statements or use incorrect grammar also appeared to be a debating weakness. Despite these perceived disadvantages, Bush acquitted himself well in the debates. Although voters did not necessarily feel that Bush defeated Gore in the debates, they seemed to develop a more favorable image of him during this period. Perhaps Bush's performance removed some of the doubts about his ability, or perhaps Gore's performance was less than what some voters expected. Whatever the reasons, Bush went from being down by several percentage points to being up by several points during this period. Had he not done so, Gore would have been the clear election winner.

The Outcome

The popular vote was close to an even split. Gore won 48.3% of the vote, slightly more than Bush's 47.8%. The electoral college vote was even closer. Bush won 271 votes, just one more than the number needed for election. Unlike every other recent election, the electoral college vote outcome was not known shortly after election day. The outcome hinged on which candidate would carry Florida, but the election results in that state could not be quickly determined. The first vote tally after the election showed Bush ahead by a small margin, but a recount of the votes, which was mandatory because of the closeness of the election, could have easily changed that. Moreover, there were questions about the election administration and vote counting in many counties, especially when it came to counting the punch card ballots used in a number of counties. Finally, the law allowed overseas absentee ballots to arrive up to ten days after election day and be legally counted.

In determining the final, official vote count, two areas generated great conflict between the Gore and Bush campaigns. One had to do with how punch card ballots were to be recounted. Gore wanted a hand recount of these ballots, at least in cases where there was a potential problem. He opposed a simple machine recount of the punch card ballots, claiming that many votes were not being properly counted by the machines, due to the problem of "hanging chads" (i.e., parts of the ballot card that should have been fully punched out by the voter but in fact were only partially detached). Bush opposed any hand recount, claiming that there were no established standards for determining how partially detached chads should be counted.

The other area of conflict involved absentee ballots, especially the overseas ballots, many of which came from members of the military (Barstow and Van Natta 2001). State law required the signature of a witness and a postmark prior to election day for a valid overseas ballot. However, many ballots arrived with no postmark, making it impossible to determine when they were mailed. The Bush campaign wanted many of these ballots to be counted, arguing that members of the military should not be disenfranchised because of oversights in the postmarking process. Democrats favored stricter standards, although Gore was cautious about pushing too far on this point, lest he be seen as taking the vote away from members of the armed forces at the same time that he was claiming that the vote was effectively being taken from many voters in punch card counties.

The political context of the conflict also was important. The Florida governor, Jeb Bush, was the brother of George W. Bush. The Florida secretary of state, who was the state official in charge of election administration, was Katherine Harris, who also was the Florida chair of the Bush campaign. Finally, the Florida legislature, which had the legal power to select the electors, was controlled by the Republicans. Given this political context, it is not surprising that Gore chose to appeal to the Florida judiciary and to the election officials in a number of the counties. These were venues that he would find more receptive to his arguments.

The legal battles went on for weeks (Ceasar and Busch 2001, 176-200). Secretary of State Harris planned to certify a winner on November 18. Had she been able to do so, Bush would have been certified as the winner by 930 votes, but attorneys for the Gore campaign obtained a state court injunction that delayed the certification. Additional recounts mandated by the courts reduced the Bush lead. On November 26, Harris certified Bush as the winner, but Gore immediately contested the certification in the state courts, arguing that many votes had still not been properly counted. Republicans took their case to the federal courts. With recounts still under way, the U.S. Supreme Court, in a very controversial decision on December 12, ordered an end to all recounts. Gore conceded the election to Bush on the following day. Bush was the official winner in Florida by about 500 votes.

Minor party candidates won much less of the vote than in the previous two elections. Less than 4% of the voters cast a ballot for a candidate other than Bush or Gore. Of those who did vote for a minor party candidate, most voted for Ralph Nader, the Green Party candidate, who won about 3% of the vote. This was not a large share of the vote, and it was well below what polls earlier in the fall had projected for Nader. Nevertheless, Nader's share of the vote was significant because it was widely viewed as coming very disproportionately from voters who otherwise would have voted for Gore. Thus, if Nader had not been in the race, Gore presumably would have had a much more substantial popular vote advantage. In Florida alone, Gore probably would have gained enough votes to put the state safely in his camp. Concerns about Nader being a spoiler led many Democrats to argue that Nader should advise his supporters to vote for Gore, at least in the states that were considered a tossup.

The congressional races were almost as close as the presidential contest (Herrnson 2001; Jacobson 2001). Republicans managed to retain control of the House of Representatives, but only by a slim margin. Democrats gained two seats in the House, leaving the Republicans with just a nine seat margin. The Senate outcome was even closer. Democrats picked up four seats, an unexpectedly large gain, leaving the Senate divided 50-50. But Republicans retained control of the Senate, even though the number of senators was evenly split between the two parties, as Vice President Cheney would be available to cast the decisive vote in the case of a tie.

Although it was a close election, it was not one that greatly excited the electorate, at least as reflected in their willingness to vote. Only around 51% of the voting age population cast a ballot in the presidential race. This rate did represent a slight increase from 1996, which had the lowest turnout since 1948, but it was well below the 55% turnout that occurred in 1992. Turnout has been on a decades-long decline, beginning in the 1960s, when nearly two-thirds of the voting age populated voted. However, it seems to have leveled out in recent years, as the turnout rate was 50% in 1988, 55% in 1992, 49% in 1996, and 51% in 2000. Of course, this leveling out is at a rate that leaves about one-half of the adult population as non-voters, hardly a desirable figure for a country that regards itself as a great democracy.

Suggested Reading

The following books are excellent discussions of the 2000 elections:

James W. Ceaser and Andrew E. Busch. *The Perfect Tie*. Lanham, MD: Rowman & Littlefield Publishers, 2001.

William Crotty (ed.). *America's Choice 2000*. Boulder, CO: Westview Press, 2001.

Michael Nelson (ed.). *The Elections of 2000*. Washington, DC: CQ Press, 2001.

Gerald M. Pomper, et al., *The Election of 2000*. New York: Chatham House Publishers of Seven Bridges Press, 2001.

CHAPTER II
ANALYZING VOTING BEHAVIOR

The most interesting questions about an election are not concerned with who won but with why the outcome occurred and what the implications of the results are. These questions are not always easily answered. Looking only at the campaign events and incidents will not suffice. The unique aspects of the election must be blended with a more general understanding of electoral behavior to create a full explanation. We thus need to discuss basic concepts and ideas used in the study of voting behavior as a basis for analyzing the 2000 results.

Two major concerns characterize the study of electoral behavior. One concern is with explaining the election result by identifying the sources of individual voting behavior. We attempt to understand the election outcome by understanding how and why the voters made up their minds. Another major concern in voting research emphasizes changes in voting patterns over time, usually with an attempt to determine what the election results tell us about the direction in which American politics is moving. In this case we focus on the dynamics of electoral behavior, especially in terms of present and future developments. These two concerns are complementary, not contradictory, but they do emphasize different sets of research questions. For our purposes, these two concerns provide a useful basis for discussing key aspects of voting behavior.

Sources of Individual Voting Behavior

On what basis do voters decide how they will cast their ballot? Several basic factors can be identified as reasons for choosing a candidate in a presidential election. A voter may choose a candidate on the basis of one or more of the following considerations: (a) orientations on specific issues of public policy; (b) general assessments of the performance of government; and (c) evaluations of the personal qualities of the candidates. When voters are asked what they like or dislike about a specific candidate—i.e., what might make them vote for or against that candidate—most of their responses fall into one of the above three categories. These orientations and evaluations in turn are influenced by two more general factors: (1) basic loyalty to or preference for a particular political party; and (2) general ideological orientations and dispositions. Party identification and ideology are more general, long-run factors that influence the attitudes that are more immediate to the vote decision in a particular year.

The various factors that influence the vote decision vary in their stability over time. Evaluations of candidate qualities and government performance are distinctly short-term forces, capable of substantial shifts from one election to the next. Party identification and ideology are much more stable in the short term. Not many voters change their party identification or ideology from one election to the next, and the changes that do occur often are fairly small ones. Issue orientations fall somewhere in between. While the specific issues crucial in presidential elections can change dramatically, as can how the voters evaluate the presidential candidates on the issues, many basic policy questions (e.g., defense spending, welfare programs, abortion) stretch across several elections, with partisan differences remaining relatively constant.

Policy Issues

The role of public policy issues in elections is of particular interest to political analysts. Elections are widely justified as providing a means for citizens to influence governmental decisions by choosing among contenders for office. The assumption often is that the electorate will shape government policy by selecting candidates on the basis of their policy stands. When this phenomenon does not appear to be the case, political commentators often are quite critical. Indeed, we frequently hear complaints that the candidates in a presidential election are failing to clearly address the real issues. Equally common are complaints that the mass media fail to adequately treat issues in their coverage of presidential election campaigns.

The term issue sometimes is used more generally to refer to anything that is a source of conflict or contention, but that is not its meaning here. We are referring to public policy issues, meaning questions of what the government should or should not do. Policy issues involve conflict over the direction of government policy. Some policy issues in an election may be quite specific, such as the conditions under which abortion should be legal. Often the policy issues are general, dealing with broad approaches to problems, such as whether the federal government should increase spending on national defense or whether social security should be privatized in some fashion.

For a policy issue to affect the vote decision, voters must have opinions on the issue and must perceive differences between the candidates on the issue. Even on important issues, many voters will fail to meet these conditions. Some will have opinions that are too weak and unstable to provide a basis for evaluating the candidates, while others will not see any significant differences between the candidates on the issue (Campbell, et al. 1960, 168-187). But some voters will have definite opinions and clear perceptions of candidate differences, particularly when the candidates clearly articulate their differences (Nie, Verba, and Petrocik 1976, 164-173). The presidential candidates in 2000 disagreed on many issues, as the first chapter outlined, although the campaign did not always stress these differences. The important question is not whether voters were provided with a choice; the question is the extent to which voters perceived candidate differences on policy issues and cast their ballots on that basis. The data for this module contain measures of both how respondents felt about a number of policy issues and how respondents perceived the stands of the candidates on some of these issues, both useful items of information for an analysis of the role of issues in the 2000 presidential election.

Government Performance

Rather than choosing among candidates on the basis of specific issues of public policy, voters may rely more on general evaluations of the performance of government. A presidential election is, at least in part, a referendum on the performance of the incumbent administration. This referendum aspect surely is present when the incumbent president is running for reelection, but it is also present even when he is not. As the Democratic candidate and the incumbent vice president, Al Gore could not avoid gaining or losing votes in 2000 in part by how voters assessed the performance and accomplishments of the Clinton administration.

Retrospective evaluations of government performance are an important determinant of voting behavior, and this effect should be distinguished from the influence of policy issues (Fiorina 1981, 3-16). Policy issues involve differences over what the government should do; they are prospective in nature. Performance evaluations involve differences over how well the government has done; they are retrospective in nature. Quite often, we find agreement over what the government should accomplish, but disagreement over how well the goals have been achieved. Basic goals such as low unemployment, low inflation, steady economic growth, national security, and world peace are shared by all. Candidates do differ in their prescriptions for economic health or national security, but discussions of the details of macroeconomic theory or of diplomatic strategies may not be followed by many voters. More relevant are general perceptions of whether the economy or national security has improved or declined.

The importance of these factors is reflected by the emphasis given to them in recent presidential elections. Republicans in 1980 sought to tie negative evaluations of the economy and the international environment to perceptions of President Carter's competence. In 1984, the Republican emphasis was on the improvement in the economy and the international environment that occurred during the Reagan administration. Similar claims were made by Republicans in 1988, while Democrats countered that everything was not so well off. In 1992, Democrats argued that President Bush was responsible for the poor health of the economy, while the Republicans claimed that the nation's economic problems were being exaggerated by the media. In 1996, the Clinton campaign highlighted the peace and prosperity of the past four years. The importance of the economy in presidential elections, especially those involving the incumbent president, is illustrated by the results of the above elections. The two presidents who were defeated, Carter and Bush, ran for reelection under unfavorable economic circumstances. The two who were reelected, Reagan and Clinton, were reelected in years in which the economy was robust.

The influence of performance evaluations on voting behavior involves several factors. First is the voter's assessment of national conditions, such as the state of the economy. Second is the voter's evaluation of government performance in dealing with the conditions. For example, a voter might feel that national economic conditions have deteriorated, but that it is not the government's fault. Also, we should distinguish between government performance in general and presidential performance in particular, at least if we are concerned with presidential elections. A voter might feel that the federal government is responsible for the poor state of the economy, but that Congress is to blame, not the president. President Bush made exactly this argument in the 1992 campaign, claiming that the Democratic Congress was responsible for the economic recession. Similarly, a voter could believe that the incumbent administration deserves little credit for a healthy economy, a claim made by many Republicans in 2000.

Economic conditions may affect perceptions of government performance, and thereby the vote, in two ways (Kiewiet 1983). One possibility is that the effect is largely a personal one, with voters reacting primarily to their own economic situation—for example, blaming the administration in power if unemployment and inflation have made their situation worse than it had been. The other possibility is that voters evaluate the economic performance of an administration quite apart from their own economic circumstances. As the economy deteriorates, people may feel that the president is doing a poor job, even if they have not personally suffered. This dataset contains information on a variety of assessments and perceptions of economic conditions and government performance, thereby allowing for an examination of the role of retrospective evaluations in voting behavior.

Candidate Characteristics

Voters also judge candidates by their personal characteristics. Included among the relevant characteristics are such things as the experience, honesty, morality, compassion, competence, and leadership ability of the candidates (Miller and Shanks 1996, 416; Page 1978, 232-265). Apart from how they see the candidates on the issues, voters form images of the personal qualities and abilities of the candidates, and these perceptions are important influences on the vote. One important aspect of personal character is the perceived honesty and trustworthiness of the candidates—what might be termed an integrity dimension. Another important dimension, which might be termed competence, involves the experience and knowledge of the candidates; in particular, voters are hardly likely to vote for someone whom they feel lacks the experience and ability to handle the job of president. A third important dimension involves the leadership ability of the candidates. Those who are perceived as strong and inspiring leaders are much more likely to be preferred by the voters. Finally, there is a compassion dimension; voters favor candidates whom they see as concerned and caring. These four dimensions of personal traits may vary in their importance; perhaps one or more of the dimensions will have little effect in any given election (Miller and Shanks 1996, 425-427).

The personal characteristics of the candidates received considerable attention in the 2000 presidential election, and both major party candidates had liabilities in this area. For example, questions were raised about Bush's experience and competence and about Gore's honesty and leadership ability.   Questions about the personal qualities of the candidates were also raised in most previous elections. Of course, almost all presidential candidates had their perceived strengths as well. In 2000, for example, many people rated Gore as very experienced and knowledgeable and Bush as very trustworthy. Indeed, Bush attempted to play to his strength by repeatedly stating that he would restore honor to the White House, a strategy based on the belief that the various scandals that emerged during Clinton's two terms would lead voters to question Gore's integrity.

It is not surprising that candidate character received considerable attention in the 2000 presidential election. Many analyses of recent presidential elections have focused on the significance of these candidate characteristics, such as honesty in 1976, competence in 1980, leadership in 1984, patriotism in 1988, and trustworthiness in 1992 and 1996. Voters seem to regard their vote for president as a very personal one, and they consider the character of the candidates seriously. Moreover, candidates have often focused on such traits when they felt that it would be advantageous to do so. The dataset contains a number of measures of respondent evaluations of candidate personal characteristics, allowing us to examine the influence of these factors in 2000.

Party Identification

Party identification is an important attitude that influences the vote. Most voters identify with one of the two major political parties, and these basic partisan loyalties influence the vote. Party identification normally is measured by asking individuals whether they consider themselves to be a Democrat, Republican, or independent. Those indicating Democratic or Republican are then asked whether they are a strong or a weak Democrat or Republican, while those claiming to be an independent are asked whether they feel closer to one of the two political parties. This yields a sevenfold classification: strong Democrats, weak Democrats, independents closer to the Democrats, independents not closer to either party, independents closer to the Republicans, weak Republicans, and strong Republicans. This seven-point party identification scale is in the dataset.

The direct influence of party identification on the vote is small in presidential elections. Very few voters probably cast a ballot for Bush solely because he was a Republican. But the indirect influence of party identification is great, in that partisan loyalties influence evaluations of candidates, assessments of government performance, and perceptions of political events. Put simply, party identification is a perceptual screen—a pair of partisan-tinted eyeglasses through which the voter views the political world. Party identification may be somewhat less important now than in the past, but it is still a very significant factor for explaining political orientations and behavior.

Ideology

Voters also tend to have general ideological orientations and dispositions. While most voters lack a well articulated and clearly thought out political ideology, most have some general tendencies. Some are strongly liberal across the board, others strongly conservative, and still others are moderates in most areas. Some may tend to be liberal in one area, such as social issues, but conservative in another, such as economic issues. These general ideological orientations influence voting (Miller and Shanks 1996, 288-294). Among Democrats, those most likely to cast a Republican ballot are those who are more conservative. Similarly, more liberal Republicans are the ones most likely to vote for a Democratic presidential candidate.

The effect of ideology on the presidential vote occurs for several reasons. Ideology affects positions on specific issues. For example, voters who are strong conservatives are likely to take conservative positions on new issues as they arise. As discussed above, positions on specific policy issues influence how voters cast their ballots in presidential elections, so this influence is one path by which ideology affects the vote. Ideology also may influence party identification, which is another path of influence. Finally, voters may have a general ideological perception of a candidate, even if they are unsure about the candidate's position on specific policy issues, and this general perception may influence their vote.

Relationships Among Attitudes

Evaluations of candidate personal characteristics, assessments of government performance, and orientations on public policy issues not only influence the vote. They affect each other. Voters who hold conservative positions on key policy issues are not only more likely to agree with the issue positions of a conservative candidate; they also will be likely to have a favorable view of the personal characteristics of that candidate. Voters who feel that the incumbent president has not managed the economy very well are likely to unfavorably judge many of the president's personal qualities, especially those regarding judgment and leadership. Although the attitudes and orientations identified above are conceptually distinct, they are empirically interrelated.

Moreover, these attitudes and orientations are shaped by party identification and ideological orientation. Party identification, as discussed above, strongly affects how voters view and interpret political events and actions. Even opinions on things that might seem fairly factual in nature, such as how well the Clinton administration managed the economy, are influenced by one's party identification. Similarly, ideological orientations and dispositions are likely to influence not only issue positions, but also perceptions of candidate characteristics and of government performance. Strong conservatives in 2000 were unlikely to think highly of Gore's personal qualities or to rate highly the economic performance of the Clinton administration. Strong liberals were likely to feel just the opposite.

Finally, while party identification usually is viewed as influencing candidate evaluations, performance assessments, and issue orientations, these attitudes may also affect party identification, especially in the long run. For example, Democrats with more conservative attitudes may become Republicans, something that clearly has been happening in the South. Similarly, voters might shift their party loyalties because of their views of government performance, especially if they consistently see one party in a more favorable light. While party identification is fairly stable, it does respond to other political attitudes.

Explaining the Vote Decision

There are multiple reasons why people vote the way that they do. The relative weight of these factors may vary among individuals. Some people vote more on the basis of the personal characteristics of the candidates, others more on the basis of issues of public policy, and still others on the basis of retrospective performance evaluations. A few may cast a ballot largely on the basis of party identification. The importance of the above factors also can vary from one election to another. While it is easy to outline the possible factors that motivate the vote, it is more difficult to specify exactly how important each factor was in determining the election outcome (Kelley 1983, 43-71).

Identifying the factors that affect the vote decision also leads to a consideration of how voters form their perceptions and evaluations. Why, for example, do some voters feel that a candidate is trustworthy, while others have the opposite opinion? What leads voters to have favorable or unfavorable assessments of government economic performance? As suggested above, party identification plays a role, but it does not fully explain the formation of these attitudes and orientations. Members of the same party often will have divergent views. While we do not have the space here for an extended discussion of this topic, it is clear that past experiences, exposure to the mass media, and political discussions with friends all play an influential role. Some of these attitudes may be determined far before the election, but others may be shaped by the campaign itself. Explaining the dynamics of opinion formation during an election is one of the most challenging aspects of electoral research (Berelson, Lazarsfeld, and McPhee 1954; Campbell 2000; Popkin 1991).

Electoral Dynamics

Election results often change dramatically. A lopsided victory for one party may be followed by a landslide for the other party in the following election. Electoral changes can be divided into two types: short-term and long-term. Short-run changes are the result of fluctuations in factors that are specific to an election, such as the characteristics of the candidates or the condition of the economy. These short-term factors may be moderately favorable to the Democrats in one election, strongly favorable to the Republicans in another, and evenly divided in a third.

Long-term shifts result from alterations in basic loyalties and represent changes that last beyond a particular election. The most significant long-term change occurs when there is a critical realignment of the party system, which refers to a relatively rapid, fundamental, and durable alteration in the pattern of party loyalties held by the electorate (Burnham 1970, 1-10; Sundquist 1983, 1-14). Realignments occur infrequently; the last major upheaval of the party system occurred in the 1930s, and before that in the 1890s and 1850s. Of course, in any time period there is some change in party loyalties, but only rarely is it substantial enough to qualify as a realignment.

The New Deal Realignment

The 1930s realignment reshaped the party system. The Great Depression acted as the catalyst for a transformation of the party system that moved the Democrats from minority to majority status at the national level. The New Deal Democratic coalition that put Franklin D. Roosevelt in the White House and the Democratic Party in control of Congress combined support from the working class and various ethnic and minority groups with already existing strength in the South. The basis of Democratic appeal to blue-collar workers, low-income individuals, and recent immigrant groups (largely Catholics and Jews from southern and eastern Europe) was the party's liberalism in economic matters. Roosevelt and the Democrats favored federal government activity to combat the Depression and proposed programs to benefit disadvantaged groups. The Republicans, who appealed more to the middle-class, business groups, and northern white Protestants, were critical of this expansion of government interference in the economy and creation of a variety of social welfare programs. By the late 1930s, the lines between the two parties were clearly drawn, both in ideological and socioeconomic terms (Ladd and Hadley 1978, 31-87).

Although the New Deal coalition began to break up in the 1960s, the impact of the New Deal realignment has remained to the present, albeit in a diluted and revised form. Many of the party images of decades past persist to the present. Democrats remain thought of as the party that favors bigger government, more spending on domestic programs, and helping those at the bottom of the economic pyramid. Republicans continue to be perceived as favoring limited government, less spending on domestic programs, and fewer restrictions on business enterprises. Democrats are seen as the party of the working class and lower-income groups. Republicans are viewed as the party of business and upper-income groups. These are not baseless images. They reflect continuing fundamental differences between the parties.

Recent Developments

The breakup of the New Deal coalition resulted from several changes in the American electorate. Most significantly, the South, which had been a bastion of Democratic strength, has now become fertile ground for Republicans, especially in national elections. The class cleavages that were so clear in the 1930s and 1940s have diminished greatly in recent years (Abramson, Aldrich, and Rhode 1999, 107-109). Union membership, a great source of Democratic strength in earlier years, has declined as a proportion of the labor force and has become less reliably Democratic in its voting (Abramson, Aldrich, and Rhode 1999, 106-107).

At the same time that some of the old partisan differences have diminished, new divisions have emerged. Beginning in the 1960s, blacks began to vote in greater numbers and to cast their ballots overwhelmingly for Democratic candidates, and they now are one of the most loyal components of the Democratic coalition of voters (Abramson, Aldrich, and Rhode 1999, 101-104). Hispanics have emerged as a significant minority group, and they generally have leaned in the Democratic direction, although not as strongly as blacks. In the 1980s, a gender gap emerged, with men more likely than women to vote Republican (Seltzer, Newman, and Leighton 1997, 31-46; Mueller 1988).

A new religious split has been developing, with Republicans appealing more to a "New Christian Right," which emphasizes traditional moral values (Wald 1987, 182-212). The older religious division between Protestants and non-Protestants (principally Catholics and Jews) was based not on theology but sociology. In the 1930s, Catholics and Jews were predominantly more recent and less assimilated immigrants from Eastern and Southern Europe, who found the Democratic Party more willing to champion their integration into American society. In the 1980s a more clearly religious dimension emerged. Fundamentalist Protestants became a more distinctly defined political group, with strong conservative leanings across a range of issues. Somewhat related to this development, Republicans in recent years have appealed more to those who are more religious, even if they are mainline Protestants and Catholics. Thus, current religious divisions involve both denomination and religiosity.

While there has been a great deal of change in recent decades, it has not added up to a critical realignment of the type that occurred in the 1930s. Nevertheless, the cumulative change over the past three decades has been substantial. Republicans have made clear gains in party loyalty during the 1980s and 1990s. While Democrats remain the majority party when it comes to identification, Republicans have greatly narrowed the margin. Moreover, Republican identifiers turn out at a higher rate than do Democratic identifiers. Among those who vote, Republicans are close to parity with the Democrats.

Change has been greatest in the South. Once solidly Democratic, the South has leaned Republican in recent national elections (Black and Black 1992, 3-28). From Reagan on, every Republican presidential candidate has run better in the South than in the rest of the nation. Republican success in southern congressional elections lagged behind the presidential victories, but beginning in 1994, a majority of southern members of Congress were Republicans. Moreover, the South has been growing more rapidly than the rest of the country, so that it has gained both congressional seats and electoral votes.

Some of the change over the past few decades could be described as dealignment. Voters have become less attached to either party, with the result being a more volatile electorate that is highly responsive to short-term forces. The diminished loyalty to parties is reflected in increased ticket splitting (voting for Democrats for some offices and Republicans for others). It also may be reflected in a greater willingness to vote for a third-party or independent candidate, such as Ross Perot. Still, the electorate can hardly be described as highly dealigned. Even if current voters are somewhat less likely than those of a few decades ago to strongly identify with a political party, the vast majority of voters have some attachment to a party and this attachment is strongly related to their voting behavior.

The combination of a more even division of partisanship with somewhat weaker partisan attachments helps to explain why divided government has been so frequent in recent years. From 1981 through 2000, one party held control of the White House and both houses of Congress for only two of the twenty years—the first two years of the Clinton presidency. Enough voters cast a presidential ballot for one party and a congressional ballot for the other to create these split outcomes.

Summary

A number of attitudinal and social factors are related to individual voting behavior. Among attitudinal factors, assessments of the personal characteristics of the candidates, evaluations of the performance of the government, orientations on specific policy issues, party identification, and ideology are the primary determinants of candidate choice. For social factors, race, religion, region, social class, and gender appear to be the characteristics most closely related to voting. Examining how these factors are related to the vote in particular elections not only allows us to explain the election outcome, but also can provide us with an understanding of electoral dynamics. All of the ideas raised in this chapter can be examined with the data contained in this package.

Suggested Readings

A good introductory discussions of elections and voting is found in the following book, which is written for an undergraduate student audience:

William H. Flanigan and Nancy H. Zingale, *Political Behavior of the American Electorate*, 9th ed. (Washington: CQ Press, 1998).

Considerable historical data on American elections are in:

Harold W. Stanley and Richard G. Niemi, *Vital Statistics on American Politics*, 1999-2000 (Washington: CQ Press, 2000).

CHAPTER III
SURVEY RESEARCH METHODS

The study of voting behavior generally relies on information from sample surveys. Aggregate election statistics from states or counties, another common type of election data, are useful for examining the patterns of election results, such as differences in the presidential vote among the fifty states, but such data are not suitable for an analysis that focuses on the individual voter. In order to investigate the factors that affect how people vote, we need information on individuals. Such information commonly includes data on voting behavior, attitudes and beliefs, personal characteristics, and so on. Since it is impractical to obtain this information for each member of the electorate, the common procedure is to draw a sample of people from the population and interview these individuals. Once collected, survey data are usually processed and stored in a form allowing for computer-assisted data analysis. Such analysis generally focuses on describing and explaining patterns of political opinion and electoral behavior. This chapter discusses the data collection procedures for sample surveys to provide the reader with the background necessary for properly analyzing and interpreting survey data.

The SETUPS Dataset

The data for this instructional package are drawn from the 2000 American National Election Study (ANES), conducted by the Center for Political Studies at The University of Michigan. This academic study is considered to be of the highest quality in all respects, including the sampling plan, questionnaire design, and interviewing. Based on a very large sample (over 1,500 people), the study interviewed respondents both before and after the election. Only a portion of all the information collected by the study is contained in this dataset, and the selected data have been prepared especially for instructional purposes.

Efficient data analysis requires that the data be recorded, coded, processed, and stored according to standard procedures. Essentially, this task involves representing all information by numeric codes, which are described in Chapter VII of this book. For example, the information that John Smith is an evangelical Protestant would be stored by recording a value of "2" (evangelical Protestant) on variable "155" (religious affiliation) for respondent "904" (John Smith). This numerically coded information usually is placed on a magnetic computer diskette or an optical compact disk, allowing the data to be analyzed with the aid of a computer. In the past, many large surveys were analyzed with larger "mainframe" computers. Now, more powerful microcomputers make it possible to analyze survey data on personal computers.

Data can be thought of as a set of information available for each respondent included in a survey. This information indicates the placement of each respondent on a number of behavioral, attitudinal, and socio-demographic factors. For example, this dataset includes information on the respondent's voting behavior in 2000 (behavioral factors), the respondent's attitudes about issues in the election campaign (attitudinal factors), and the respondent's gender, race, and education (socio-demographic factors). Each of these factors can be termed a variable. A variable is simply some factor for which there is a set of values (at least two) such that each person has some specific value (i.e., position or categorization) on that variable. Thus the respondent's gender would be a variable, and "male" and "female" would be the two possible values for that variable.

Some variables, such as the respondent's gender or religious affiliation, clearly have a limited number of possible values. These are categoric variables. Other variables, such as the respondent's family income (expressed in dollars per year) can assume any value along a range of possible scores. These variables can be termed continuous. Of course, a continuous variable can be made into a categoric variable by grouping or categorizing the responses. For example, this was done to income by recoding the respondent's family income into five categories (less than $15,000, $15,000 to $35,000, $35,000 to $65,000, $65,000 to $85,000, and $85,000 or more). Similarly, a categoric variable with many possible responses can be regrouped into fewer response categories. For example, we simplified the religious affiliation variable by placing the many possible religious denominations into a few broad categories (see V155). Most of the variables in the dataset for this module have a small number of possible values. This was done to make the data easier to analyze using contingency tables. The exceptions to this rule are a set of continuous variables (V201-V222) that were left in their original form so that instructors who wanted to use more advanced statistical techniques, such as multiple regression, could do so.

In order to use a dataset, a codebook is needed. The codebook describes the dataset by providing a list of all variables, an explanation of each variable, and a description of the possible values for each variable. The codebook also indicates how the data are stored and organized for use by the computer. A codebook can thus be thought of as a combination of a map and an index to the dataset. The codebook for this dataset is located in Chapter VII. Detailed information for the use of the codebook is in Chapter VI.

Survey Sampling Plans

Analyzing the data for this instructional package involves making generalizations and drawing conclusions about the American electorate from the set of people who were interviewed in the survey. Fortunately for social scientists, it is possible to study large populations by examining samples drawn from these populations. Of course, it is not possible to estimate perfectly the characteristics of a large population (e.g., American adults) from a sample of 1500 individuals, but such a sample can provide a reasonably accurate representation of the larger population. However, it is also possible for the data from a sample survey to be inaccurate, and it is desirable to have some understanding of the potential sources of error in the data before engaging in data analysis. Very basically, errors in a sample can be divided into two different types—systematic error and random error. The goal of proper sampling is to reduce *both* of these, but, as we will see, the first is a much more serious—although more easily addressed—problem than is the second.

The degree to which a sample is likely to represent some larger population depends most heavily on the sampling procedure used to isolate the sample. If we attempted to study all American adults by having interviewers stand on selected street corners and interview some of those passing by, then we probably would not obtain a sample that faithfully represents the entire population. First of all, the people who walk by street corners where the interviewers are may differ significantly from those who do not. Second, the interviewers may consciously or unconsciously choose certain types of people to interview. Both of these are sources of systematic error in the sample. To improve our chances of obtaining a more representative sample, a different sampling plan is necessary, one that does not automatically exclude certain members of the population and does not allow for any selection bias from the interviewers. This sampling plan is one that would dramatically reduce the systematic error that existed in the plan described above.

The most basic form of sampling that reduces systematic error is the simple random sample, which involves randomly drawing a sample from a list of all members of the population. For example, if we want a sample of 500 students from the undergraduate body of 15,000 at a large university, we could obtain the names of all undergraduate students from the university registrar, put each name on a slip of paper, put all the slips of paper in a hat (a *very* large hat!), shake the hat to mix up the names, and draw a sample of 500 names from the hat. This procedure would guarantee that every individual in the population of 15,000 had the same chance of being included in the sample as every other individual and that the choice of any one individual did not affect the chance that any other would be chosen. These procedures are the keys to random sampling. Of course, hats are not necessary to select random samples; computers can easily be programmed to take a random sample of a population by generating a series of random numbers that are assigned to the population.

While simple random sampling is appropriate for some situations, it is not generally appropriate for most social science research applications. In the case of the university sample, we would probably want to make sure that the sample of 500 students contained relatively the same percentage of freshmen, sophomores, juniors, and seniors as were in the university under-graduate population of 15,000. A simple random sampling procedure would not guarantee such a distribution. By luck we might obtain a sample that had too many freshmen or too few seniors. A more complicated sampling procedure that would guarantee that the classes were represented according to their weight in the population is called stratified probability sampling. To take a stratified probability sample of the university, we would first divide the names obtained from the registrar into freshmen, sophomores, juniors, and seniors, and put each set of names into its own hat. We would then need to determine what percentage of the population fell into each of the four classes. Suppose we know that 30% of the undergraduate population are freshmen, 27% are sophomores, 23% are juniors, and 20% are seniors. To reflect accurately these percentages in the sample, we would need 150 freshmen, 135 sophomores, 115 juniors, and 100 seniors. The actual selection of the individual names for the sample would be conducted in the same manner as for a simple random sample. We would randomly select 150 names from the freshman hat, 135 from the sophomore hat, 115 from the junior hat, and 100 from the senior hat. The resulting sample not only reflects the underlying percentages of students in each of the four classes at the university, but is also true to the principles of random sampling identified above. Again, the hat is unnecessary; a computer can easily be programmed to supply the random numbers needed to take the sample.

Modern survey research essentially applies these and other principles in its sampling procedures. Simple random samples are impractical in national studies for two basic reasons. First, there is no national list of all American adults; second, the sample would be scattered all over the country, making it very expensive to send interviewers out to each respondent, if face-to-face interviews are being used. For these reasons, a more complicated type of probability sample is normally drawn in national studies in such a way that the sampling procedure is as unbiased as the simple random sample and an improvement on it in other respects.

The sampling procedure used to conduct a representative national survey depends on whether one is conducting a telephone survey or a face-to-face survey. One commonly used method for drawing national samples for telephone surveys is to identify all of the area codes in use in the U.S., then identify all of the exchanges in use in each area code. After this is done, a computer is programmed to dial a four digit random sequence of numbers which is added to each of the telephone exchanges in each of the area codes. The actual number of respondents in any area code is determined by the actual number of telephone numbers assigned in the geographic area for which that area code is used. One major advantage of this "random digit dialing" technique is that it allows for people whose telephone numbers are unlisted in any telephone directory to be included in a survey. A major disadvantage to pure random digit dialing is the large number of calls that must be made to get a valid interview. Many calls are made to businesses or to unassigned phone numbers. Typically, five calls must be made to get one working residential phone. Because of the large number of calls that need to be made to obtain valid interviews, most survey organizations modify pure random digit dialing and use sampling techniques that attempt to minimize this problem and so keep their costs within reasonable bounds. One widely used variation on pure random digit dialing that dramatically increases the odds of getting a residential phone number is known as the Waksberg method, used by the Survey Research Center at the University of Michigan (Weisberg, Krosnick and, Bowen 1996, 53-61).

The chief advantages of telephone interviewing over face-to-face interviewing are cost and convenience. It is simply very costly to send interviewers out into the field to conduct interviews. Interviewers operating in the field on their own must be superbly trained to handle all kinds of interview situations. Telephone interviewing only requires a bank of telephones with interviewers at each one. All of the interviewers are in one place and can be carefully supervised by a well-trained supervisor. While face-to-face surveys are more difficult to conduct and more expensive than phone surveys, they usually yield richer data since the interviewer can ask a variety of follow-up questions, can spend adequate time to make the respondent feel comfortable in answering questions about sensitive information, and can note any circumstances about the interview that the interviewer thinks might have affected the answers given.

Sources of Errors in Surveys

Even in a survey of high quality, some error will be present. Some of the error will be random sampling error, which is the error introduced by the sampling procedure itself—i.e., from interviewing a sample of the population rather than every person. Random error can also come from accidental errors by interviewers or coders. In addition to the random error, there will be systematic error. There may be some systematic bias to the sample, for any sampling plan tends to exclude certain remote and inaccessible types of people. For example, the Survey Research Center sampling plan used by the American National Election Study excludes residents of Alaska and Hawaii. Systematic error can also result from questioning individuals. For example, certain questions may have an unrecognized bias to them, so that respondents tend to respond in a particular way even if they feel differently.

Regardless of how well-designed the sampling procedure is, it is necessary to have a reasonably large sample in order to have confidence that the sample is representative of the population. Even if the finest sampling plan is used, a sample of ten people almost surely will be unrepresentative as a result of chance alone. But if a sample of 1,000 individuals is chosen by the same procedure, then it is very likely that the sample will be quite representative, as the random factors are likely to even out in a larger sample. Thus, we want to have both a well-designed probability sampling plan and a large sample size. Of course, a large sample will be more expensive than a small one, as interviewing costs are a major part of a survey.

The presence of random sampling error means that the results obtained by the study must be taken as close approximations of the population rather than perfectly precise representations. For example, if 75% of the people interviewed in the study said that they were in favor of spending more federal money on public schools, it would be incorrect to conclude that exactly 75% of all American adults felt that way. The true population figure should be about, but probably not exactly 75%. For a sample of 1500 respondents, the random error introduced by the process of sampling alone will be less than 3 percentage points 95% of the time. In other words, if our sample shows that 75% of the people favor increasing expenditures on public schools, then we would be very confident that the true population figure is between 72% and 78% (i.e., 75% -3% and 75% +3%). Naturally, the sampling error will be larger for a smaller sample, or when a subset of a larger sample is used, and less for a larger sample. The existence of random error means that we must pay attention to the total number of respondents that our conclusions are based on.

Interviews are never obtained from every individual selected in the sample. Some will refuse to be questioned, and, more likely, others will not be at home when the interviewer calls. Interviewers can call back to obtain interviews from those who were not at home originally, but some will never be home when an attempt is made to contact them. The problem caused by these "refusals" and "not-at-homes" is that those who are not interviewed may differ in some fundamental ways from those who are interviewed. A trivial example of this problem is a survey in which all interviews are planned for daytime hours. This would systematically exclude most working people. We might then expect to get a very different distribution of answers on questions about the importance of government programs to handle the problem of child care than if we had a survey in which some people were called in the evening. This potential source of bias will be a more serious problem when the non-response rate is high, so survey researchers try to minimize the number of non-responses. This usually means having the interviewers make repeated callbacks and interviewing at different times of the day, both of which increase the cost of the survey.

Failure to reach the respondent is only one reason why interviews are not obtained from all respondents. A second, and potentially more serious, reason is simple refusal to cooperate with the survey interview. All survey interviews, of course, require the cooperation of the individual who is being interviewed. If the individual refuses to answer any questions at all or refuses to continue an interview that has already begun, information cannot be obtained from the respondent. Partially as a result of the increasing number of surveys conducted by industry, polling firms, and academic researchers, the number of people refusing to be interviewed in recent years has increased dramatically. One writer has termed the large number of refusals survey research's "dirty little secret" (Van Natta 1999). If people who refuse to be interviewed are somehow different--in terms of partisan identification, ideology, or a variety of other orientations--from those who agree to be interviewed, refusal can become a source of systematic error.

The actual effects of this survey fatigue are open to question. Reputable survey research organizations recognize that the increased rate of refusals is a problem, and so they make additional efforts to garner cooperation from potential respondents up to an including using special interviewers to convince non-respondents to cooperate with the survey (Traugott and Lavrakas 2000). And some recent research has also demonstrated that low response rates in exit polls at the precinct level, for example, is "unrelated to the accuracy of the survey in predicting the actual election outcome in the precinct" (Traugott and Lavrakas 2000, 68). Nevertheless, the potential bias introduced when a large number of people refuse to participate in survey research is a source of concern to those who conduct such research.

The process of obtaining information from the survey respondents by having interviewers administer questionnaires is another potential source of error. The respondents may be less than candid on some points, the interviewers may make mistakes, and some questions may be misleading. For example, if a survey of all American adults finds that 5% of the respondents stated that they cheated on their income tax, it would be foolish to conclude that in reality only one American in twenty engages in this practice, for there is the very real possibility that many of the respondents did not answer the question truthfully. Many voting studies have found that respondents over-report having voted in the last election. When reported voting behavior is compared to actual voting behavior through voter validation studies, which examine the official board of elections records, somewhere around 10% of respondents erroneously report having voted when they actually did not (Katosh and Traugott 1981).

Other errors occur when respondents are not consciously being untruthful but simply have forgotten what a past behavior was, or when respondents mistakenly interpret a survey as some kind of test of their knowledge of or involvement in politics. For example, some early voting studies found that a substantial number of respondents changed their opinions on public policy issues over a short period of time; further investigation showed that many of these respondents really did not have opinions but gave answers anyway since they did not want to appear uninformed to the interviewer (Converse 1964, 1970; Converse and Markus 1979). Systematic error can result from poor question wording, which can encourage respondents to express an opinion on an issue when they do not have one. One way to minimize this type of error is for experts in the fields of public opinion and survey research to review questions for content, presentation, and interpretation. A second way is to ask questions in different forms to subsets of the sample and then to compare the results that are obtained via the different ways the questions were worded. The American National Election Study uses these methods in the design of the survey, and, as was stated above, this year's study directly experimented with different question formats in different delivery modes. Nevertheless, we rarely can know exactly how much systematic error, if any, is present for a specific item. We should, therefore, be sensitive to the fact that on some types of questions some respondents will not be truthful or accurate.

One question regarding survey research that has plagued researchers for years is that of the comparability of data gathered in face-to-face interviews and data gathered in telephone interviews. The 2000 ANES sample was developed partially to answer this question. The designers of the survey questionnaire experimented with different ways to ask various questions, and then varied these question word-ings across the face-to-face and telephone samples. The primary purpose of this experiment was to examine whether the way the question is worded and the format in which it is asked influence the type of answers respondents give. The results of this experiment will be analyzed by researchers for years. One practical problem that this experiment caused, however, is exactly how to use the data generated by two different types of question wording. In developing the dataset for this instruc-tional package, we have assumed that the data generated by telephone and face-to-face interviews using the same or highly similar questions can be combined into a single item. In some cases, however, the face-to-face and the telephone versions used questions that were not sufficiently similar, at least in our opinion, to justify treating the two questions as essentially the same item. In these cases, the dataset contains two different questions, each asked of about one-half of the respondents, to measure the same attitude.

The information recorded by the interviewers may not be a perfect reflection of the true opinions and behavior of the respondents. However, if a well-designed questionnaire and well-trained interviewers are used, this type of error can be held to a minimum. Skilled interviewers are less likely to make careless errors in asking questions and recording information. A well-designed questionnaire will have each question worded in a clear and unbiased manner, which will help to produce accu-rate results. Again, minimizing error involves some cost. Extensive prior testing of the questionnaire before actual use involves expenditures of time and money, as does careful selection and training of interviewers. It is clear that while the prin-ciples for obtaining a good survey are well known, practical considerations place limits on the application of these principles. A survey research organization gener-ally has a fixed sum of money for conducting a particular study, and this financial limitation may dictate that some procedures be done in less-than-ideal fashion. High quality surveys will cost more, but the information collected will be more accurate.

In sum, it is important to be aware of the potential sources of error when working with survey data. Fortunately, the error present in a well designed and conducted survey will be minimal in most cases. It therefore is possible to draw meaningful and valid conclusions from an analysis of survey data. At the same time, it is necessary to realize that there can be some differences between the true behavior and opinion of a population and what the survey shows the behavior and opinions to be.

The ANES Data

The 2000 American National Election Study (ANES) used two different survey methodologies and two different sampling frames. The first was a face-to-face study of 1,006 respondents interviewed before the 2000 presidential election, with 694 re-interviewed after the election (also using face-to-face interviews). The second was a telephone study which interviewed 803 respondents prior to the election and 862 respondents after the election. Some of those who were interviewed face-to-face before the election were interviewed by telephone after the election, which explains why there is a higher number of telephone post-election interviews than telephone pre-election interviews.

The national sample for the face-to-face surveys was drawn by an area probability method, which relies on U.S. Census figures and maps of the country. The ANES used a four-stage process to draw its national sample. This process, called a multistage area probability sample, is based on a methodology developed at the Survey Research Center at The University of Michigan and the National Opinion Research Center at The University of Chicago. The first stage of this process for the 2000 study involved selection of main or "primary" sampling units from the listing of all Metropolitan Statistical Areas (MSAs), single non-MSA counties, and groups of small non-MSA counties. Second stage sampling involved selection of second-stage sampling units, either census blocks (in urban areas) or enumeration districts (in more rural areas), from the primary stage units isolated in stage one. In stage three, listings of all housing units located in the physical boundaries of the second-stage sampling unit were made, and a sample of housing units within each sampling unit was taken. In stage four, all adults in a household were identified and one was selected on a random basis (Weisberg, Krosnick, and Bowen 1996). The procedures for identifying who should be interviewed are objective; the interviewers are not allowed to replace somebody they are supposed to interview with somebody else. Because of the care taken in selecting the sample and training interviewers, systematic error is minimized. The only systematic error in this sampling plan would come from inaccuracies in the information supplied from the U. S. Census or errors in actually implementing the procedures.

The telephone component of the 2000 ANES used random digit dialing and employed the Waksberg, method mentioned earlier to select the survey sample. The technical term for this method is a stratified equal-probability sample of telephone numbers. This type of sampling does not simply generate random telephone numbers, since such a method of sampling would be extremely inefficient (some area codes are not assigned; within a given area code, some exchanges are not used–000, for example; and within a given exchange, some specific numbers are not assigned or are retained for future assignment). Thus, the sample was selected in the following fashion. To begin, the first seven digits of the ten-digit telephone numbers (the three-digit area codes, three-digit exchanges, and the first digit of the last four numbers) were selected. Next, the remaining three digits were selected randomly, using the criterion that at least two telephone numbers must have been assigned from a given bank of one hundred numbers. For example, if no telephone numbers had been assigned out of the 100-199 bank for a given set of seven initial digits, this bank would be ignored in the random selection of remaining digits.

This procedure resulted in an initial sample of 8500 telephone numbers for the coterminous 48 states. These numbers were pre-screened by the commercial vendor with whom the Survey Research Center worked to remove most business and non-working phone numbers. After pre-screening, 5,760 or 67.8% of the 8500 telephone numbers were identified as potentially working residential numbers. These potentially working phone numbers were matched against a file of directory listings so that Congressional District could be assigned. Before the final sample was selected, the telephone numbers were stratified according to how competitive the Congressional race was (5 levels were used), whether or not the race had an incumbent or was open, and by US Census Division (Census Divisions are groupings of states that subdivisions of the four Census regions—Northeast, South, Midwest, and West). Half of this sample was selected through systematic sampling, and eventually a final sample of 2,349 cases was selected. The remaining telephone numbers were assigned to a reserve grouping to be used if response rates in the initial sample became too low.

All the respondents were interviewed in the fall of 2000 before and after the election by highly trained interviewers, using either telephone or face-to-face interviews. The response rate for the pre-election survey was approximately 64% for the face-to-face sample and 56% for the telephone sample. Response rates for the post-election study were approximately 86% for both the face-to-face and telephone samples. This dataset includes the 1555 respondents interviewed in both the pre-election phase (September or October) and the post-election phase (November or December). You should be aware that the attitudes of some voters could have changed between the time they were first interviewed and the time they cast their ballot. You should also remember the unusual characteristics of the 2000 presidential election; as a result of the closeness of the popular vote and questions concerning the way voting was conducted and counted in the state of Florida, the winner was not known until a month after election day. Post-election interviewing was being conducted when the winner—George Bush—was announced.

The data for this instructional module are weighted. Weighting a dataset is a technical procedure in which each respondent counts as more or less than one case, depending on the value of the weight assigned to that respondent. The data for this instructional module are weighted to correct for several basic factors—the two samples used in the study, larger versus smaller households, and attrition from the pre-election to post election interviews. The resulting weighted data set contains 1554, rather than 1555, respondents since it was impossible to get the weighted sample to be exactly 1555. You should not be overly concerned about weighting in the dataset, since the dataset is designed to be automatically weighted when you open it. For the most part, the weighting is transparent—you will not even notice that you are working with weighted data.

Suggested Reading

Herbert F. Weisberg, Jon Krosnick, and Bruce Bowen, *Introduction to Survey Research, Polling and Data Analysis,* 3rd edition (Newbury Park, CA: Sage, 1996).

CHAPTER IV
PRINCIPLES OF DATA ANALYSIS

Reports of surveys or polls in the popular media describe behavior or opinion, usually reporting such things as the proportion of people who favor some proposal, who feel a certain way, or who have engaged in some activity. These reports deal with what are often called the "what" questions of social science research—for example, what does the American public think about abortion? However, research in political science is concerned with more than mere description of data. The emphasis is on analysis and explanation, or "why" questions—for example, why did some people vote for George Bush in 2000 while others voted for Al Gore? Answering such questions involves examining relationships among variables.

Relationships Between Variables

Two variables are related to each other when certain values of one variable are likely to be associated with certain values for the other variable. Conversely, two variables are unrelated when the values of one variable are equally likely to be associated with any of the values for the other variable. For example, if we say that education and turnout (i.e., whether one votes) are related, this could mean that more educated people are more likely to vote (which is what we would expect), or that more educated people are less likely to vote. Either way, the two variables would be related, for values on one variable would be linked to values on the other variable. Naturally, it would be far more informative to state how education and turnout are related, rather than just state the simple fact that they are related, and this should be done whenever possible. When speaking about the relationship between two variables, the terms independent variable and dependent variable are commonly used. The independent variable can be considered to be the "cause" and the dependent variable the "effect." In other words, the independent variable affects or influences the dependent variable. A common research procedure is to start with some dependent variable and then to identify some independent variables that are strongly related to the dependent variable. In this way the dependent variable is explained, at least in the sense that some of the factors that influence it are identified.

When analyzing survey data, a common procedure is to use a contingency table. A contingency table presents the cross-tabulation between two variables (tables with three or more variables are possible, but we shall refer only to the more basic table for now). A cross-tabulation refers to the pattern of joint occurrences for the two variables. By examining a contingency table, it is possible to determine whether or not two variables are related. For example, Table IV-1 is a contingency table that presents the cross-tabulation between party identification and presidential vote. One variable, the respondent's party identification (divided into seven categories) is at the top of the table, with one column for each of the seven values for the variable. The other variable, presidential vote, is along the side of the table with one row for each of the two values of the variable (those voting for minor party

candidates are excluded from this table). The seven columns and two rows inter-
sect to form fourteen cells.

The fourteen cells of Table IV-1 correspond to the possible categories that a
respondent could fall into. A respondent could be a strong Democrat who voted for
Gore, an independent Democrat who voted for Bush, and so on. The number in
parentheses in each cell indicates the total number of respondents who fall into the
category (e.g., there were 176 respondents who were strong Republicans and who
voted for Bush). The numbers on the right side and the bottom of the table are
called "marginals," and they indicate the total number of respondents in each row
or column. The number in the lower right corner (n = 1050) is the total number of
respondents included in the table.

TABLE IV-1 Presidential Vote by Party Identification

Party Identification

Pres. Vote	Strong Dem.	Weak Dem.	Indep. Dem.	Indep.	Indep. Rep.	Weak Rep.	Strong Rep.	
Bush	3.0%	14.6%	22.4%	54.5%	85.2%	83.6%	98.3%	47.7%
	(7)	(24)	(30)	(42)	(115)	(107)	(176)	(501)
Gore	97.0%	85.4%	77.6%	45.5%	13.8%	16.4%	1.7%	52.3%
	(226)	(140)	(104)	(35)	(20)	(21)	(3)	(549)
	100.0%	100.0%	100.0%	100.0%	100.0%	100.0%	100.0%	N =
	(233)	(164)	(134)	(77)	(135)	(128)	(179)	1050

$Tau_c = -.84$

Respondents who did not vote as well as the few who voted for somebody
other than Bush or Gore are not included in this table, so the total is less than the
1554 in the sample. The 504 individuals who are not in Table IV-1 all show "missing
data" on one or both of the variables that compose the table. As noted, missing
data occur in the interview situation for one of three reasons: the question does not
apply to the respondent (e.g., people who did not vote were not asked which
presidential candidate they voted for), the respondent refused to give an answer or
had no opinion on the issue, or the interviewers failed to obtain the information for
some other reason.

In order to interpret contingency tables, it is desirable to convert the cell
frequencies into percentages. The usual way to calculate percentages in a contingency table is by each category of the independent variable, which is usually
placed at the top of the table, as it is here. Since party identification clearly is the
independent variable in this case, the percentages have been calculated by column
(i.e., each column totals to 100%). If the independent variable were placed at the

side of the table, the percentages would have been calculated by row (i.e., each row would total to 100%). For example, Table IV-1 shows us that 85.2% of the 135 independent Republicans voted for Bush while 14.8% voted for Gore. According to the data in Table IV-1, strong Democrats were the most likely to vote for Gore and strong Republicans the least likely, with the other groups basically arranged between these two extremes. While the overall tendency is clear, we should not treat each of the percentages as a perfect reflection of the true population figure, since we are dealing with a sample. Thus, it would be better to say that, for the country as a whole, *around* 85% of the independent Republicans cast a ballot for Bush.

This simple example illustrates the basic ideas behind reading and interpreting contingency tables. The general rule is to compare categories of the independent variable in terms of the percentage distribution on the dependent variable. If the independent variable is the column variable (as in Table IV-1), then percentages should be calculated by column and the entries in the columns compared. A proper observation drawn from Table IV-1 is that the percentage of voters reporting having voted for Gore goes down dramatically when we move from the strong Democrat column (97.0%) to the strong Republican column (1.7%). Likewise, the percentage of voters reporting having voted for Bush goes up dramatically when we move from the strong Democrat column (3.0%) to the strong Republican column (98.3%), with the sole exception that independent Republicans (85.2%) report having voted for Bush slightly more frequently than did weak Republicans (83.6%).

In comparing column entries, the focus should be on looking for differences, and one should note the size of the difference identified. Very small differences should be treated as insignificant, on the grounds that these small differences could be the result of random error and are probably not meaningful anyway. Where the difference are large enough to be considered real, it is important to note how strongly the variables are related. For example, in Table IV-1 we can see that the differences among Democrats, Republicans, and independents in their presidential voting is substantial (about 97% of strong Democrats voted for Gore; about 45% of independents voted for Gore; and only about 2% of strong Republicans did so). If the difference between strong Democrats and strong Republicans were only about ten percentage points, we would classify the relationship as a weak one. And if there were virtually no differences at all in the percentage distributions in each column, then we would say that no relationship existed. We should also pay attention to the total number of respondents that the column percentages are based on. If there are too few cases in a column, the percentages in the column cannot be regarded as reliable. As a general rule, we should be cautious in interpreting percentages when there are fewer than 50 respondents in the column (note that we are referring to the column, not the cell!), and when there are fewer than 20, we should be extremely cautious in any interpretation.

Useful Statistics

To measure the strength of relationships more precisely, statisticians have developed various "measures of association" that can be calculated for a table. Many different measures of association have been designed, but most of these statistics share some general characteristics: they are equal to zero when there is no relationship, and they increase as the relationship becomes stronger, until they reach a value of 1.00 for a perfect direct relationship (or -1.00 in some cases where a perfect inverse relationship exists). However, you will not encounter any perfect relationships with these data. The relationship in Table IV-1 is one of the strongest to be found in the 2000 data.

One commonly used statistic is Kendall's tau. This measure of association is appropriate when we have variables that are ordinal, meaning that their categories form a logical order or progression, such as from high to low or from liberal to conservative. Any variable with only two categories can be considered ordinal. For example, if we had a table showing the relationship between education (an ordinal variable) and turnout (which has two categories--voted and did not vote), tau would be an appropriate statistic to determine the strength of the relationship between the two variables. It would equal zero if more educated and less educated individuals voted at the same rate, and it would equal one if all the more educated people voted and all the less educated people did not vote. For situations between these two extremes, tau would be somewhere between zero and one. For larger tables (tables with, for example, four columns and four rows), tau will equal +1.0 only when all cases are on the major diagonal of the table--that is, the only cases in the table are in the cells that start in the upper left hand corner of the table and proceed diagonally to the lower right hand corner. Rectangular tables (where the two variables have different numbers of categories) do not have clear diagonals. For this reason, some statistical packages (such as SPSS) report Kendall's tau-b to be used with square tables and Kendall's tau-c to be used with rectangular tables. Other statistical packages report only tau-c, since the result of calculating tau-c for a square table will be very similar to tau-b.

When we have ordinal variables, we frequently refer to positive (direct) and negative (inverse) relationships. A positive relationship exists when the changes in the independent variable are associated with changes in the same direction for the dependent variable. A negative relationship exists when we have the reverse; changes in one variable are associated with opposite direction changes in the other variable. Tau and other statistics appropriate for ordinal variables will assume negative values in these cases. Of course, whether a relationship is positive or negative depends on how the variables are defined; by reversing the coding of one of the variables we change the direction *but not the magnitude* of the association. The important thing to do is to examine the table to see the direction of the relationship and to use the statistics to determine the strength of the relationship.

Table IV-1 illustrates these points. The table displays the two-party presidential vote (a variable recoded to have only two values) by party identification (a variable with seven values). Party identification is an ordinal variable and the two-party presidential vote is a variable with only two categories. Tau-c is thus an appropriate statistic to be calculated for this table. The highly negative tau calculated for Table IV-2 can be interpreted as meaning that there is a strong relationship between party identification and the two-party presidential vote--as one identifies more strongly with the Republican party, one's tendency to vote for Bush increases. The negative tau and gamma calculated in Table IV-1 could, of course, become positive if we reversed the order of the codes of *either* party identification *or* presidential vote. The current party identification scale runs from 1 = "Strong Democrat" to 7 = "Strong Republican." If we reversed this by recoding the data so that the scale ran from 1 = "Strong Republican" to 7 = "Strong Democrat," the tau calculated for Table IV-1 would be +.84. Likewise, if we recoded presidential vote such that 1 = AGore@ and 2 = ABush@ (the reverse of what it is in Table IV-1) and crosstabulated this variable against the *unrecoded* party identification variable, the tau would be +.84. Reversing *both* party identification *and* presidential vote would, of course, result in a negative tau. We will have more to say about recoding data in a later section of this chapter.

When the variables are nominal (i.e., there is no logical order to the categories), either Cramer's V or the contingency coefficient are appropriate measures of association. For example, if we had a table showing the relationship between religious affiliation and presidential vote, Cramer's V would be appropriate; it would equal one if we could predict the presidential vote perfectly simply by knowing the person's religion (e.g., if all mainline Protestants voted one way, all evangelical Protestants another way, and so on), and it would equal zero if each religious group voted in the same manner. The contingency coefficient could also be calculated for this table and would yield similar results.

In addition to tau, Cramer's V, and the contingency coefficient, there are many other statistics for use with contingency tables. Other commonly used statistics for ordinal variables are gamma and Somer's d, and lambda or phi are other commonly used statistics for nominal level variables. We shall leave it up to your professor to suggest which measures of association, if any, you should use. The great value of these statistics is that they can summarize in a single number an entire table with many cells and percentages. On the other hand, a disadvantage of summary statistics is that they summarize the relationship. In doing so, some detailed information about the relationship is lost.

Remember that measures of association do not really tell you any more than percentages in the table, they just do it more conveniently. Also remember that most measures of association can be calculated on any data you might have. It makes little theoretical sense to relate presidential vote to the length of the respondent's first name, and yet there is nothing in any computer routine that would stop you from doing so! Nor do computer routines stop you from calculating ordinal level statistics on data that are nominal, or vice versa. Whether the measure you select is appropriate (and therefore useful) for the data you calculate it on, and whether the relationships you investigate make theoretical sense, are matters of your own substantive knowledge of voting behavior and methodological training in data analysis.

Statistical Packages and Data Analysis

The survey data for this instructional package can be analyzed according to the above principles. The specific computer commands and methods for generating the desired contingency tables will depend somewhat on the local computing environment, but most students will be using SPSS (Statistical Package for the Social Sciences), a popular Windows-based microcomputer statistical package. There are other statistical programs, such as SAS, Stata, or Microcase., that could be used, but we have chosen to provide instructions for SPSS because it the most widely used statistical package in political science courses.

In SPSS, only a small number of commands are necessary to generate the desired analysis. The *crosstabs* command would be used to generate the tables in the exercises in Chapters IV and V of this monograph. When using *crosstabs*, you should specify the variables as "dependent variable by independent variable." This will produce tables with the independent variable across the top (defining the columns) and the dependent variable along the side (defining the rows). The command used to generate Table IV-1 is:

crosstabs tables=v002 by v008/cells=counts col.

This command shows the basic syntax of *crosstabs*. In addition to specifying the table through the use of the variable numbers (V002 is presidential vote in 2000; V008 is party identification), the commands tells SPSS to print the actual number of cases in each cell of the table (counts) and to print the column percentages (col) in each cell. This command should be entered in the syntax window of SPSS for Windows.

Box IV-1: Using Menus in SPSS for Windows

Many users may prefer to conduct the analysis described here using the pull-down menus available in SPSS. While it is somewhat difficult to describe the process for doing so here without having the Windows program running, we will nevertheless attempt to do so.

The **crosstabs** *in SPSS is available in the* **analyze** *menu which is on the toolbar at the top of the screen. Highlight* **analyze** *and then highlight* **descriptive statistics**. *On the* **descriptive statistics** *menu, highlight* **crosstabs**. *You will see a window in which you can specify the variables you wish to crosstabulate. To move a variable into the column or row category, simply click on the variable and click on the appropriate arrow. Remember that in this monograph we are treating the independent variable as the column variable and the dependent variable as the row variable.*

Before actually building the table you desire (by clicking on the **OK** *box), you will need to specify that you want column percentages to be reported in your output. This is done by clicking on the* **cells** *box at the bottom of the screen and then the* **column percentage** *and* **continue** *boxes. If you want to specify any statistics to be calculated on the table, this can be done by clicking on the* **statistics** *box and then clicking on whatever statistics you would like to see.*

When you have the table set up the way you want, click on the **OK** *box and your computer will construct the table you specified. The table will appear in the SPSS output window, which should come up automatically after SPSS finishes executing the* **crosstabs** *command.*

All of the analysis described in this chapter can be accomplished by using either the pull down menus (as described in this box) or by typing the commands in the SPSS syntax window (as described in the text). We have emphasized using the syntax windows commands in the text because it saves time in the long run if one will be analyzing the data over several sessions. The syntax file from the previous session can be saved and modified for the next session. Also, by printing out the syntax file from each session, one will have a record of exactly how variables were coded and what tables were requested during that session, which often is very useful.

Recoding Variables

Although the variables in this instructional dataset have been coded into what we think are the most logical categories, there are times that you might want to change the coding. For example, we have coded education (V149) to have six categories (not a high school graduate; high school graduate only; some college but no degree, some college with an AA degree, college graduate, and advanced degree). Although these represent logical categories, there are at least two good reasons why one might want to recode the education variable. First, you may think that the real distinction in education is between those people who have not gone to college and those who have (even if people who went to college did not graduate). Second, you might find that there were too few cases in some of the six categories to allow you to make valid conclusions about the differences that exist between columns in a table. If either of these were the case, you could recode the education variable into two categories instead of six by "collapsing" those who have a "1" or a "2" on education into "1" and renaming this category something like "HS Only." Those with a "3," A4,@ "5," or a A6" on education could then be collapsed into a "2" and renamed something like "Any College." Another possibility would be to recode education into three categories by combining the first two categories (those who have a high school education only), the middle two categories (those who have some college, but not a four-year degree), and the last two categories (those who are college graduates). Which method of recoding education is better depends on the educational distinctions that you think are important.

Recoding can have theoretical overtones. Let use examine party identification (V008). V008 is coded here on a seven-point scale, which runs from Strong Democrat to Strong Republican, with independent being the middle category. For some uses, the seven-point scale simply has too many categories and results in tables with too few respondents for meaningful analysis. Recoding V008 into a smaller number of categories would increase the number of individuals in any one cell of a table and therefore might be desirable here. There is some controversy, however, about exactly *how* party identification should be recoded. Party identification is assessed through answers to three questions: First respondents are asked whether they generally consider themselves to be Democrats, Republicans, or independents. For those who call themselves Democrats or Republicans, the strength of their attachment to their party is then asked. Those who call themselves independents are asked whether they feel closer to the Republicans, Democrats, or to neither party.

Recoding party identification into three categories (Democrat, independent, Republican) would result in large numbers of respondents in each category, but at the sacrifice of the strength of respondents' attachment to their political party. Nevertheless, we could accomplish such a recoding easily enough, as long as we decide beforehand who is a Democrat, who is an independent, and who is a Republican. The particular problem here concerns those who originally called themselves independents but then say that they are close to either the Democratic or Republican party. There are two alternative treatments that can be used here. First, we could stay with the initial question sorting and treat all those who originally called themselves independents as independents in the recoded variable. Our coding scheme would thus combine all those who are originally a "1" or "2" into "1"

(Democrat), all those who are originally a "3," "4," or "5" into "2" (independent), and all those who are originally a "6," or "7" into "3" (Republican). Alternatively, we might consider the fact that independent Democrats and weak Democrats are usually very similar in their presidential voting, as are independent and weak Republicans (Wattenberg 1994, 25-26). In fact, in some years independent Democrats have actually voted slightly more heavily Democratic than have weak Democrats, and a similar pattern is true for the Republican side (this is true for Republicans identifiers in 2000 but not for Democratic identifiers--see Table IV-1). We might then want to combine independent Democrats in with the weak and strong Democrats, and the independent Republicans in with the weak and strong Republicans. This second coding scheme combines all those who are originally a "1," "2," or "3" into "1" (Democrat), all those who are originally a "4" into a "2" (independent), and all those who are originally a "5," "6," or "7" into a "3" (Republican). Needless to say, there would be large changes in the numbers of respondents in each of the three categories depending on which coding scheme was used. You can see from this example that the jury is still out on how party identification should be recoded.

Recoding party identification is a fairly easy process in SPSS or most other computer-based statistical packages. In SPSS, we could recode party identification (V008) in the first way proposed above with the following commands:

> **compute v008r=v008.**
> **recode v008r (1,2=1) (3,4,5=2) (6,7=3).**
> **variable labels v008r 'Recoded Party Identification'.**
> **value labels v008r 1 'Democrat' 2 'Independent' 3 'Republican' 9 'NA'.**

This series of commands does several things. First, it creates a new variable (V008r) which is the equivalent of V008. V008r is then recoded into three categories. You should note that immediately following the *recode* command, we have assigned a variable label to V008r and have reassigned value labels for recoded party identification.

These commands show several good data analysis habits to develop. First, create a new variable to recode, rather than recoding the original variable. When an original variable is recoded, it remains so for the rest of the computer run in which you make the change, and thus it is impossible to "recapture" the original unrecoded variable in the same computer run. Creating the new variable allows you to keep the original unrecoded variable while working with a new recoded one. Second, assign variable labels to new variables as soon as you create them. It is often clear what you want to do in a computer run when you are doing it, but later when you examine the printout from the run, your intentions may be less clear. Naming a variable when it is created will help you to keep things straight. Third, assign value labels immediately after creating the new variable. It can become confusing to have recoded variables without value labels. While SPSS does not require you to provide labels for recoded variables, any tables that you generate using unlabeled variables will be more difficult to read, especially if you are not sure exactly how you recoded the variables.

For the second party identification recoding scheme described above, the SPSS statements would look very similar to those above, but would be:

> **compute v008r=v008.**
> **recode v008r (1,2,3=1) (4=2) (5,6,7=3).**
> **variable labels v008r 'Recoded Party Identification'.**

value labels v008r 1 'Democrat' 2 'Independent' 3 'Republican' 9 'NA'.

You should note here that, although the value labels are the same as those in the first recode command above, the number of cases that will go into each category will be different. Specifically, here we are calling more respondents Democrats and Republicans (and fewer respondents independents) than we do above. If you wanted to experiment with *both* ways of recoding party identification in the same computer run, you could create two new variables that were the equivalent of party identification (V008) but with different variable numbers (V008r1 and V008r2, for example) and recode them in the two ways described. You would want to assign descriptive variable labels to these two new variables in order to differentiate between them.

Conclusion

The necessary instructions for using computers at your school to analyze the data supplied with this instructional package will be supplied by your professor. Your school's computing environment and your professor's experience with computer-based instructional packages will determine which package you use to work on the exercises in Chapter V. Although we have used SPSS to illustrate the commands for cross-tabulation and recoding, it is certainly not the only computer-based statistical package that can be used to complete the exercises in Chapter IV. If another statistical package is used, the commands for cross-tabulation and recoding will be different than those shown above.

CHAPTER V
ANALYSIS EXERCISES

In the last chapter, the computer commands necessary to generate Table IV-1 were described. In order to proceed with this instructional package, it will be necessary for you to generate your own tables in like manner as Table IV-1 was generated. The first two exercises in this chapter will allow you to make sure that you can properly obtain the tables you want; you can check your results against the tables in this chapter to verify your understanding of the appropriate computer procedures. The exercises also will require you to apply the principles of table reading that were discussed in the previous chapter. These elementary exercises will then be followed by more complex ones that involve more sophisticated techniques. Last, we will suggest some further projects that you might want to conduct on your own.

Part A: Two-Variable Relationships

Most analyses of survey data begin with a look at relationships between two variables. These "bivariate" relationships are often followed by analyses that look at the relationships among three or more variables ("multivariate" relationships). Before discussing multivariate analysis, it is important to have a clear understanding of the principles of bivariate analysis. In the following exercise, you will be creating a table that is analogous to Table IV-1. We will begin by looking at the relationship between presidential vote and how the respondent assessed recent changes in the national economy.

Exercise One

Using the computer-based statistical package available to you, obtain a table showing the relationship between the two-party presidential vote in 2000 (recoded V002) and V063 (the respondent's view of the economy last year). You should be able to determine which of these two is the independent variable, which is the dependent variable, and how to lay out the table. The correct table is reproduced below as Table V-1. You can check the table you generated against it to make sure that you properly requested the table.

This table is organized so that the independent variable runs across the top and the percentages are calculated by column, which is the customary arrangement, as discussed in Chapter IV. The table has V063 at the top, as the independent variable, because it makes sense to think that how a person assessed how well the economy performed last year may have affected how he or she voted, not the other way around.

Before going on with Exercise One, make sure you understand Table V-1 and the commands you used to generate it. By examining and comparing the column entries and the marginal figures, you should be able to answer the following questions:

Table V-1:

Table V-1: Presidential Vote by Evaluation of National Economy in Last Year

Evaluation of National Economy in Last Year

Presidential Vote	Much Better	Somewhat Better	About the Same	Somewhat Worse	Much Worse	
Bush	24.3% (34)	34.7% (93)	55.4% (270)	67.7% (21)	69.1% (85)	48.0% (503)
Gore	75.7% (106)	65.3% (175)	44.6% (217)	32.3% (10)	30.9% (38)	52.0% (546)
	100.0% (140)	100.0% (268)	100.0% (487)	100.0% (31)	100.0% (123)	N = 1049

Kendall's Tau$_c$ = -.31

1. Overall, what percentage of respondents in the table voted for Bush? What percentage voted for Gore? How does this percentage compare with the national figure obtained from actual vote counts (refer to Chapter I for the election results)? What might explain any differences you find?

2. How many respondents in the table were in each of the five categories of V063? Is this the kind of distribution you would have expected for this question? Does it match the numbers in the codebook? If not, why not?

3. What percentage of the respondents who had a very positive view of the economy voted for Gore? How does this compare with the percentage voting for Gore in the other categories? How would you describe the overall relationship between these two variables?

Before beginning Exercise Two, it will be necessary to review measurement levels, something that was introduced in Chapter IV. Variables can be measured in a number of different ways. Some variables are nominal variables, meaning that the possible values do not form any order at all. Marital status (V147) is an example of this type of variable. The possible values (married, single, divorced, etc.) do not form any order. The numbers assigned to the values could be changed (divorced could be coded as "1"; married as "2") without hurting the measurement scheme at all. Other variables are measured on an ordinal scale, meaning that the possible values for the variable have an implicit order. Education (V149), as measured in this instructional dataset, is an ordinal variable, since the possible values can be arranged from low to high (or from high to low). A person who has just a high school education has less education than a college graduate, but more than someone who is not a high school graduate. Still other variables might be measured on an interval scale, meaning not only is there an implicit order to the variable, but the intervals between the categories are assumed to be equal. If age had been measured by actual age in years, it would have been an interval level variable. Moving from 33 to 34 years of age would be the same as moving from 56 to 57 years of age, as in both cases the change involves one year of age. You will not need to worry much about interval level data in this dataset since the only interval level variables are those that have been included in a special section designed for instructors who want to use more advanced statistical techniques, such as multiple regression.

Exercise Two

The independent variable in Exercise One is an ordinal variable, and in looking for a relationship between that variable and the two-party vote we are looking for a tendency for Bush's support to increase (or Gore's to decrease) as we go from left to right across the columns in the table. In other words, we are looking for more than simple differences across the columns; we have a hunch that there is a certain order to the differences–specifically, that those who thought the economy had gotten better over the last year will vote more heavily for Gore. If we found, for example, that those in the middle category on V063 in Table V-1 voted most strongly for Gore, it would have been less clear what the relationship between the two variables really is. It would make much more sense to think that voters who felt the economy was the same as a year ago would be: (1) *less* likely to vote for Gore than those who felt the economy was better than a year ago, and (2) *more* likely to vote for Gore than those who felt the economy was worse than a year ago.

Exercise Two involves a situation in which the independent variable is a nominal-level variable. Look at V147 (marital status). Since there is no implicit order to this variable, we consider it to be nominal level. Obtain a table showing the relationship between the two-party vote for president (recoded V002) and marital status (V147). Again, you should be able to set up the table properly, and you can check your results with those in Table V-2.

Table V-2: Presidential Vote by Marital Status

	Marital Status				
Presidential Vote	Married	Single	Divorced, Separated	Widowed	
Bush	53.4% (359)	36.6% (74)	40.4% (44)	36.8% (25)	47.8% (502)
Gore	46.6% (313)	63.4% (128)	59.6% (65)	63.2% (43)	52.2% (549)
	100.0% (672)	100.0% (202)	100.0% (109)	100.0% (68)	N = 1051

Cramer's V= .152

In this case, we are interested in seeing if there are any differences among the columns in terms of the two-party presidential vote. There is no particular expectation that the columns are ordered in terms of degree of support for either Gore or Bush. Examine the table and attempt to answer the following questions:

1. What differences do you see in the two-party presidential vote among people of different marital statuses? How would you describe the relationship in Table V-2? Is it a strong or a weak relationship?

2. Are the results in Table V-2 what you expected? How would you attempt to explain the findings? Why would Bush (or Gore) do better among people who were married, single, widowed, or divorced?

We also could run the above table without recoding V002, which would show the relationship between what the respondent's marital status and the respondent's vote, including those who preferred candidates other than the two major party candidates. But remember that fewer than 4% of the voters preferred such candidates. This means that the number of cases in the cells making up the row of those voting for other candidates will be extremely small.

Part B: Three-Variable Relationships

The first two exercises were designed to familiarize you with the technical procedures for obtaining tables from your computer facilities and to explain the basic ideas of reading contingency tables. However, simple bivariate relationships frequently are only the starting point for an analysis. They often raise as many questions as they answer, and further (usually multivariate) analysis generally is necessary to explain why the bivariate relationship exists.

Exercise Three

Often, analysts of voting behavior and elections want to explain how individuals vote on the basis of certain policy issues—those who show more conservative positions on these issues might be thought to vote for Republican candidates while those who show more liberal positions might be thought to vote for Democratic candidates. One such issue in the late 1990s has been whether government of vouchers should be used to fund education. The argument for vouchers says that, at least in some situations, government should provide parents of school-age children with a monetary voucher that the parents could then use to pay their child's tuition and fees at whatever school the parents chose. Competition for vouchers would lead schools into improving their educational offerings. Those opposed to vouchers claim that such a plan would destroy public education as we know it today and would also discriminate against poorer and minority families, who might be the last ones to "spend" their vouchers and thus be forced to choose between the least desirable schools. Opposition to school vouchers also comes from those who believe that using such vouchers at schools with a religious affiliation would violate the constitutional principle of a separation of church and state activities.

This instructional dataset includes a question about school vouchers (V096). Exercise Three involves the relationship between positions on school vouchers and vote in the 2000 presidential election. In order to accomplish this exercise, begin by obtaining a table that shows the relationship between position on school vouchers (V096) and the two party vote (recoded V002). From the exercises above, you should be able to properly format this table. Table V-3 shows the results you should have obtained. You can check your results against Table V-3 to make sure you have correctly formatted the table.

Table V-3:	Presidential Vote by School Vouchers		
	Position on School Vouchers		
Presidential Vote	Favor	Oppose	
Bush	57.0% (256)	41.8% (174)	49.7% (430)
Gore	43.0% (193)	58.2% (242)	50.3% (435)
	100.0% (449)	100.0% (416)	N = 865
Kendall's Tau$_c$ = .15			

By examining Table V-3, you should be able to conclude that those who favored school vouchers had about a 15 percentage point greater propensity to for Bush than those who opposed vouchers. Is this a "real" example of issue voting or is there something else that might be influencing this relationship? There is ample evidence that issue positions vary according to party identification, and we might argue that those who consider themselves to be Democrats would generally be opposed to school vouchers and also would vote for Gore, while those who consider themselves to be Republicans would generally be in favor of school vouchers and also would have voted for Bush. Of course, there is no necessary link between the party identification and one's position on school vouchers. A Democratic identifier might still be in favor of school vouchers and a Republican identifier might still be opposed. But overall we might expect that there would be a tendency for these two variables (party identification and position on school vouchers) to be related, and this might explain our original relationship. Thus, we might hypothesize that attitude on school vouchers has no direct effect on the vote, and that the relationship between these two variable simply is due to their connection to party identification.

We can see if the data support or refute our hypothesis by constructing a three-variable table. In this case, we will want to look at the relationship between V002 (recoded to give us the two-party vote) and V056, controlling for V008. Controlling is a method of removing or separating the effects of another variable. In the example before us, we seek to remove the effects of party identification (the control variable) to see whether or not there is a direct relationship between positions on school vouchers and presidential vote. We do this by: (1) dividing respondents into the different categories of the control variable; and (2) looking at our original two-variable relationship within each of the categories. This allows us to look at the relationship between our independent and dependent variables for a set of people who are similar in terms of the control variable. Since V008 has seven categories (ranging from strong Democrat to strong Republican), it would be wise to recode it first into three categories–Democrats, independents, and Republicans. This recoding will increase the number of respondents in each subtable and make the analysis easier to interpret. As we discussed in the previous chapter, there is more than one way to recode party identification. In this case, we suggest recoding all those with any Democratic inclination into one category, and similarly for Republicans, leaving only pure independents in the middle category.

You should obtain a three-dimensional table relating V002 (recoded) to V096, controlling for V008 (recoded). This three-variable table will consist of three subtables, one for each of the three subcategories of party identification (Democrat, independent, and Republican). The three subtables are included below as

Table V-4: Presidential Vote by School Vouchers (Democrats)

	Position on School Vouchers		
Presidential Vote	Favor	Oppose	
Bush	13.8% (26)	9.4% (22)	11.4% (48)
Gore	86.2% (162)	90.6% (211)	88.6% (373)
	100.0% (188)	100.0% (233)	N = 421

Kendall's Tau$_c$ = .07

Table V-5: Presidential Vote by School Vouchers (Independents)

	Position on School Vouchers		
Presidential Vote	Favor	Oppose	
Bush	58.3% (14)	54.1% (20)	55.7% (34)
Gore	41.7% (10)	45.9% (17)	44.3% (36)
	100.0% (24)	100.0% (37)	N = 61

Kendall's Tau$_c$ = .02

Table V-6: Presidential Vote by School Vouchers (Republicans)

Position on School Vouchers

Presidential Vote	Favor	Oppose	
Bush	91.1% (215)	89.8% (132)	90.6% (347)
Gore	8.9% (21)	10.2% (15)	9.4% (36)
	100.0% (236)	100.0% (147)	N = 383

Kendall's Tau$_c$ = .02

Tables V-4 through V-6, to allow you to check your results.

In examining Tables V-4 through V-6, compare the results to Table V-3 and answer the following questions:

1. How does the relationship between V096 and V002 in Tables V-4 differ from what exists in Table V-3?

2. Examine the relationship between V096 and V002 in Tables V-5 and V-6. How are the results similar to those in Table V-4? Be sure to concentrate on the differences between columns *within* each table, not just the absolute percentage differences from table to table. Also look at the magnitude of the Tau$_b$ in the tables.

3. How does Bush's support change as you move from the first subtable to the second? Why should this be the case?

4. Looking at the subtables, can you determine the relationship between V008 (recoded) and V096? Are these two variables related? (Hint: focus on the marginal distribution for each subtable.)

5. Overall, how do these results support our original hypothesis? Explain your answer.

This example is one where the original relationship basically disappears when a control variable is introduced; the difference between the column percentages within each of the three sub-tables is *much* smaller than the difference between the column percentages in Table V-3. When this occurs, it tells us that we have found an explanation for the relationship. If the relationship had remained, the explanation that we hypothesized would have been refuted by the data. Either way, the analysis results would have told us something useful. One basic reason for introducing control variables into the analysis is to test explanations for why two variables are related.

In this case, we controlled for what we hypothesized was an extraneous variable--i.e., one that influences both of the variables in our original relationship. This is the situation where the original two-variable relationship represents a "spurious" relationship produced by the action of an extraneous variable. Controlling for the extraneous variable in this situation causes the original two variable relationship to disappear. The original relationship might also disappear (or fail to disappear) through the actions of a potential intervening variable, one that forms a link between the independent and dependent variables. Exercise Four addresses this situation.

Exercise Four

A gender gap has been the topic of a number of analyses of recent presidential elections. Women have repeatedly been more likely to vote Democratic than have men (alternatively, we could say that men are more likely to vote Republican than are women). We can analyze the gender gap in the 2000 presidential election by starting with the relationship between recoded V002 (the two-party presidential vote) and V144 (gender). Obtain this table and answer the following questions:

1. What association, if any, exists between these two variables?
2. How would you explain the results you obtained?

We might think that the gender gap was the result of some attitude on which women and men differed and which also was related to how they voted. For example, one might hypothesize that women were more likely to vote for Gore because of their attitude on abortion. That is, women preferred Gore because he was "pro-choice," whereas men preferred Bush because he was "pro-life." Consider how the relationship between gender and the vote might change if you controlled for one's attitude toward abortion (V087). Obtain a three-dimensional table showing V002 (recoded) by V144 by V087 (you will need to recode V087 into two categories–those opposed to abortion and those in favor of it in order for there to be a sufficient number of cases in each category for these tables to make sense). Carefully examine the two subtables you obtained and answer the following questions:

1. What is the relationship between V002 and V144 in the two subtables? Is the relationship between gender and the vote stronger or weaker than what we observed in the original two-variable table? Be sure to concentrate on the tendency, not the absolute percentages.
2. Would you have predicted these results? Why or why not?

These results test for the existence of a potential intervening variable. In this situation, the potential intervening variable does not have much effect .The relationship between gender and the vote remains fairly strong even when we control for the effects of positions on abortion. Thus, the data do not support our hypothesis that the gender gap in the 2000 presidential election was a result of attitudes on abortion.

Part C: More Three-Variable Relationships

One does not always control for a third variable to explain why two variables are related. Sometimes we are interested in seeing whether the relationship is stronger for some groups of people than for others. Such information often helps us more thoroughly understand the behavior we are examining.

Exercise Five

Our next exercise goes more into detail on the gender gap and is intended to stimulate your thinking for further work. It is also intended to illustrate further reasons for examining multivariate tables.

What could help us explain and understand the gender gap? In Exercise Four, we found that the gender gap is not due to positions on the issue of abortion. In Exercise Two, however, we found that there is a big difference in how people of various marital statuses vote. Could we develop a better understanding of the gender gap by looking at the differences or similarities between men and women of different marital statuses? In order to do this, you will need to obtain subtables for the two-party vote (V002 recoded) by gender (V144) by marital status (V147). The first of these four subtables (for married people only) is included below:

Table V-7: Presidential Vote by Gender
(Married People)

Presidential Vote	Gender		
	Male	Female	
Bush	55.5%	51.5%	53.4%
	(176)	(183)	(359)
Gore	44.5%	48.5%	46.6%
	(141)	(172)	(313)
	100.0%	100.0%	N =
	(317)	(355)	672

Gamma = .08

Although we have presented only one of the subtables, you should generate all four of the subtables necessary to examine the relationship between gender, marital status, and the vote. In examining these subtables, what differences do you see between married men and women, single men and women, divorced men and women, and widowed men and women? Are any of these four groups similar to each other in terms of their vote in the 2000 presidential election? Can you think of any issues that might cause the gender gap in voting to vary by marital status? The impact of marital status on the relationship between gender and the vote might suggest why gender and voting are related. Determine which additional variables you might want to introduce into the analysis to examine further the relationship between gender and the vote, and obtain the proper tables to examine this relationship. A good place to start would be to obtain tables for whatever public policy issues you think might be relevant by gender and by marital status. These will tell you if there are, indeed, gender and marital status differences on these issues. After looking at these tables, three-way tables will need to be generated and analyzed. After doing so, see what conclusions you draw concerning the nature and sources of the gender gap. Would you say that the gender gap is a result of "women's issues," or is the explanation more complex? Can you explain why there is only a small difference in voting between married men and women?

One might, of course, be interested in differences in the political orientations of men and women other than how each group voted. Survey evidence dating back to the 1930s shows a difference between men's and women's positions on foreign affairs. For example, the number of women supporting U.S. involvement in the Gulf War was twelve percentage points lower than the number of men supporting such involvement, and women were some sixteen percentage points more likely than men to think that U.S. use of the atomic bomb to end the World War II was morally wrong (Erikson and Tedin 1995). Differences between men and women also exist for domestic issues. Stouffer (1955) found that men had a somewhat higher level of support for civil liberties than did women. More recently, Shapiro and Mahajan (1986) found that women support a more compassionate approach to policy issues than do men, displaying more enthusiasm for government programs aimed at helping the disadvantaged. An excellent brief description and explanation of gender differences can be found in Erikson and Tedin (1995; pp. 208-212).

Exercise Six

A substantial number of voters in the 2000 election were ticket-splitters–individuals who voted for Gore for President but for Republican candidates for Congress or for Bush for President but for Democratic candidates for Congress. How can we examine the nature and sources of ticket-splitting? This exercise takes up this topic.

In order to look at the topic of ticket-splitting, it will be necessary to determine how many voters actually split their tickets in the 2000 election. Table V-8 addresses this question by showing the relationship between the two party presidential vote (recoded V002) and House of Representative vote (V004). In this table, we can see that some 81% of Gore voters voted for the Democratic candidate for Congress while a slightly higher percentage–about 82%–of Bush voters also voted for the Republican candidate.

Table V-8: Presidential Vote by Congressional Vote

	Presidential Vote		
Presidential Vote	Bush	Gore	
Republican	81.9% (313)	18.7% (80)	48.6% (393)
Democrat	18.1% (69)	81.3% (347)	51.4% (416)
	100.0% (382)	100.0% (427)	N = 809

Tau$_b$ = .63

We might think, however, that there are a number of factors that could influ-

Prix du Public - Audience Award
Festival du Film de SUNDANCE Film Festival

Un nouveau film du co-réalisateur de
A new film from the co-director of   **MANUFACTURING CONSENT**

★★★★
Geoff Pevere, Toronto Star

★★★★
Katherine Monk, Vancouver Sun

« Le prochain
BOWLING FOR COLUMBINE »
(Globe and Mail)

"The next
BOWLING FOR COLUMBINE."
Globe and Mail

the
Corporation
un film de Mark Achbar, Jennifer Abbott et Joel Bakan

Mettant en vedette : 7 PDG, 2 VICE-PRÉSIDENTS, 2 DÉNONCIATEURS, 1 COURTIER, 1 ESPION et 1 ÉNORME FOUILLIS
AVEC LA PARTICIPATION SPÉCIALE DU CONSULTANT EN CHEF DU FBI POUR LES PSYCHOPATHES

Avec/With MICHAEL MOORE, NOAM CHOMSKY, NAOMI KLEIN et/and MILTON FRIEDMAN dans leur propre rôle/as themselves

STARRING 7 CEOS, 3 VPS, 2 WHISTLEBLOWERS, 1 BROKER, 1 SPY, AND 1 REALLY BIG MESS
SPECIAL GUEST STAR: THE FBI'S TOP CONSULTANT ON PSYCHOPATHS

Réalisation/Directed by MARK ACHBAR Productions/Produced by MARK ACHBAR and BART SIMPSON Montage/Edited by JENNIFER ABBOTT Scénario/Written by JOEL BAKAN Textes et narration/With Narration Written by HAROLD CROOKS and MARK ACHBAR Narration/Narrated by Mikela J. Mikael
D'après le livre/Based on the book THE CORPORATION: The Pathological Pursuit of Profit and Power par/by Joel Bakan Co-producteurs/Co-Producers CARI GREEN, NATHAN NEUMER, TOM SHANDEL Responsable oeuvres de commande à TVO/ TVO Commissioning Editor RUDY BUTTIGNOL
Producteurs associés/Associate Producers JOEL BAKAN and DAWN BRETT Recherche d'archives/Archival Researcher PAULA SAWADSKY Conception sonore et supervision musicale/Sound Designer & Music Supervisor VELCROW RIPPER Bande originale/ Orginal Music LEONARD J. PAUL Musique par/Music by YO LA TENGO, DAVID WILCOX,
LIZUMNE TAIKO, TRANSMO, THIRD EYE, SHAWN PINCHBECK, MORGAN/NELKEN, ANDY MCNEILL, THE MAZEGUIDER, LOUD, LOSCIL, JEREMIAH KLEIN, HIGHER INTELLIGENCE AGENCY & BIOSPHERE, INTERMISSION, GRAMMY 'ARK, DOMAKESAYTHINK, SEAN O. ANDREWS, MITCHELL AKIYAMA, ACCENT MUSIC PRODUCTIONS
Directeur des communications centrales/Director of Corporate Communications KATHERINE DODDS, GOOD COMPANY COMMUNICATIONS Création/Created by MARK ACHBAR and JOEL BAKAN Producteur exécutif/Executive Producer MARK ACHBAR

Produit par Big Picture Media Corporation en association avec TV ONTARIO, Vision TV, Knowledge Network, Saskatchewan Communications Network et ACCESS – The Education Station. Produit avec la participation du Fonds canadien de télévision, Téléfilm Canada : Programme de participation au capital, FCT : programme des frais de permis,
British Columbia Film, Fonds canadien du film et de la vidéo indépendants, Rogers Documentary Fund, Rogers Telefund et Film Incentive BC de la province de Colombie-Britannique. Produit avec l'aide du Programme du crédit d'impôt pour producteur cinématographique ou magnétoscopique canadienne. Produit en partie grâce à des dons
d'Yvonne Tasker-Rothenberg et du Martin Rothenburg Fund, du Simon Fraser Institute for the Humanities, de la Baag Foundation et d'Istar Pares. Remerciements particuliers à Nick Prolonger. © BIG PICTURE MEDIA CORPORATION MMI

www.thecorporation.com

Opens April 23 / En salle le 23 avril

Montréal	Montréal	Montréal	Québec
Cinéma du Parc	**Cinéma Parallèle**	**AMC Forum 22**	**Cinéma Cartier**
3575 Avenue du Parc	3536 boul. Saint-Laurent (514) 847-2206	2313 Ste-Catherine Ouest	1019 avenue Cartier (418) 522-1011
(514) 281-1900	v.o. avec sous-titres français	(514) 904-1250	v.o. avec sous-titres français

the Corporation

un film de/a film by Mark Achbar, Jennifer Abbott et Joel Bakan

"Cogent, entertaining, even rabble-rousing indictment of perhaps the most influential institutional model of our era"

« Une critique intelligente, divertissante et même provocatrice de ce qui est peut-être le modèle d'institution le plus influent de notre époque. »

Dennis Harvey, Variety

Over forty interview subjects - from CEOs and corporate insiders to critics, whistleblowers and rabble-rousers - comprise a portrait of an institution with incredible power… and a few cracks in its armour.

Plus d'une quarantaine de personnes furent interviewées pour ce film: des PDG, des analystes corporatifs, des critiques et autres dénonciateurs qui dressent avec leurs témoignages le portrait d'une institution qui détient des pouvoirs exceptionnels… mais dont l'armure n'est pas infaillible.

Volunteer! Send an email. Sign up NOW.
Appel aux bénévoles! Inscrivez-vous MAINTENANT.
www.thecorporation.com

Pass this leaflet on! / Faites circuler ce dépliant!

Errata Sheet--Correction in Table V-8: Dependent variable is <u>Congressional Vote</u>.

One might, of course, be interested in differences in the political orientations of men and women other than how each group voted. Survey evidence dating back to the 1930s shows a difference between men's and women's positions on foreign affairs. For example, the number of women supporting U.S. involvement in the Gulf War was twelve percentage points lower than the number of men supporting such involvement, and women were some sixteen percentage points more likely than men to think that U.S. use of the atomic bomb to end the World War II was morally wrong (Erikson and Tedin 1995). Differences between men and women also exist for domestic issues. Stouffer (1955) found that men had a somewhat higher level of support for civil liberties than did women. More recently, Shapiro and Mahajan (1986) found that women support a more compassionate approach to policy issues than do men, displaying more enthusiasm for government programs aimed at helping the disadvantaged. An excellent brief description and explanation of gender differences can be found in Erikson and Tedin (1995; pp. 208-212).

Exercise Six

A substantial number of voters in the 2000 election were ticket-splitters–individuals who voted for Gore for President but for Republican candidates for Congress or for Bush for President but for Democratic candidates for Congress. How can we examine the nature and sources of ticket-splitting? This exercise takes up this topic.

In order to look at the topic of ticket-splitting, it will be necessary to determine how many voters actually split their tickets in the 2000 election. Table V-8 addresses this question by showing the relationship between the two party presidential vote (recoded V002) and House of Representative vote (V004). In this table, we can see that some 81% of Gore voters voted for the Democratic candidate for Congress while a slightly higher percentage–about 82%–of Bush voters also voted for the Republican candidate.

Table V-8:	Presidential Vote by Congressional Vote		
	Presidential Vote		
Congressional Vote	Bush	Gore	
Republican	81.9% (313)	18.7% (80)	48.6% (393)
Democrat	18.1% (69)	81.3% (347)	51.4% (416)
	100.0% (382)	100.0% (427)	N = 809

$Tau_b = .63$

We might think, however, that there are a number of factors that could influ-

ence whether a person would cast a straight ticket ballot or a split ticket ballot. Among these factors most likely would be the type of House of Representatives race that the individual voter experienced in his or her district. The typical percentage of incumbent US Representatives who are returned to office in biennial elections is about 95%, thus indicating that a number of people are crossing party lines to vote for the incumbent, regardless of whether he or she is a Republican or Democrat. Thus we might think that obtaining a three way table that looks at the relationship between presidential vote and congressional vote controlling for the type of US House race (V005). By now, you should be able to obtain these tables, format them properly, and interpret them. After doing so, answer the following questions:

1. How does the relationship between presidential vote and congressional vote vary according to the type of congressional race?

2. Are there substantial differences in the tau statistic between the three sub-tables? How would you explain these differences?

You might want to think of other reasons that some people split their tickets while others do not. What kind of influence do you think that party identification (V008) might have on this relationship? Would you think that strong partisans might be the least likely to split their tickets while weak partisans might be more likely? What kind of influence do you think that past voting behavior (V003) might have on this relationship? Would you think that people who had voted for Bob Dole, the Republican candidate for president in 1996 and also voted for Bush in 2000 might be less likely to vote for Democrats for the House of Representatives in 2000? What about the approximately 8% of the voters who voted for Ross Perot in 1996? Would you think ticket splitting might vary by the region of the country in which the individual lived? You should be able to construct the necessary tables and obtain the proper statistics to answer these questions in the dataset that accompanies this monograph.

Part D: Testing Your Own Theory

One way of studying voting behavior might be to have the computer generate all possible tables that could be constructed from these data. Such a strategy is neither practical nor useful. Tables by themselves tell you very little. They have to be interpreted and explained. This interpretation usually is done in terms of some theory or generalization about how people behave.

To make research efforts more meaningful, and to avoid wasted effort, we need to carefully frame the question we are studying and to be sure that we have some sound reason for studying it. That reason usually is directly related to some theoretical concepts or ideas that we have learned from the work of others. The general rule is to apply what we already know to discover something new.

It is important to explicate why we are looking at a particular set of relationships, because that justification becomes part of the explanation of what the contingency tables tell us. Political scientists are far more interested in the relationship among variables than they are in the actual percentages of some group that voted one way or another. Relationships help to explain behavior. We especially want to know why the variables are related the way that they are. We also want to know why two variables that our theory predicts *should* be related might wind up not to be related when we look at the data. Often, the lack of a finding or the fact that two variables are unrelated is just as important as finding that two variables are strongly related, but only when we have a pre-existing theory or hypothesis that predicts that the two variables should be related.

Most research involves hypothesis testing. We start from a theory developed by reading other people's work; we generate hypotheses from that theory; and we test those hypotheses by comparing our predicted relationships to those resulting from data analysis. If the data bear out our hypotheses, we can claim some support for the theory; if the data do not bear out our hypotheses, we can conclude that the theory is not supported. In either event, the conclusions are valuable.

Using what you already know about voting behavior, as well as your intuition, design a short research project that examines some aspect of voting behavior or public opinion. Specifically, you should (1) formulate a question about the relationship among a set of variables; (2) justify the selection of variables and the expectations you have about the connection between the variables; (3) test your ideas by obtaining the necessary tables; and (4) carefully interpret the tables and write up your conclusions.

Although this text has tended to focus on one dependent variable--who people vote for--the research project described above could involve other dependent variables. One might be interested in issue differences between men and women, as suggested above, or in why people think one candidate for office is honest and another one is not, or in what attributes respondents are considering when they report feeling "warm" or "cool" towards a candidate for office on a feeling thermometer. The data set associated with this monograph contains a wealth of variables that can be considered as either dependent or independent variables according to the type of research project your are pursuing.

CHAPTER VI
USER INFORMATION

The data for this instruction package are drawn from the 2000 American National Election Study, a large national survey conducted by the Center for Political Studies at the University of Michigan. These data have been substantially modified for classroom use and represent only a portion of the 2000 American National Election Study. The survey waves interviewed before and after election day are the sources of the data for this package. Only the 1555 respondents who were interviewed both before and after the election are included in this dataset, which was produced with the cooperation of the American Political Science Association and the Inter-university Consortium for Political and Social Research.

Using the Codebook

The codebook provides both a description of the data and information necessary for using the data. Every available variable is listed in the codebook, and the entry for each variable contains the information needed to use the variable in the data analysis. Below is a sample codebook entry, with each specific item of information identified by the description that points to it. An explanation of each item of information follows the sample entry. This sample entry applies to the first 160 variables (V001 to V160), all of which are categoric variables. A set of twenty-two interval-level variables (V201 to V222) are discussed at the end of this chapter.

Sample Codebook Entry

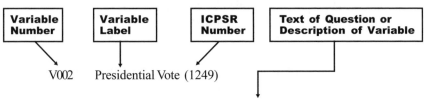

V002   Presidential Vote (1249)

Whom did you vote for in the presidential election?

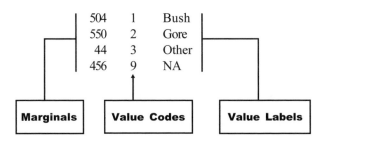

504	1	Bush
550	2	Gore
44	3	Other
456	9	NA

Explanation of Codebook Information

1. ***Variable number.*** Each variable in the dataset has been assigned a unique number, which is preceded by the letter "V" (for variable). This use of variable numbers provides a simple shorthand way of referring to variables in the dataset. Note that each number is always three digits (e.g., V002, not V2), so that the variables will be listed in proper numerical order by SPSS.

2. ***Variable label.*** Each variable has been given a unique label. If SPSS is used for the data analysis, the tables generated will have the appropriate variable labels printed on them as a convenient aid. Certain other statistical packages also will provide variable labels. Because there are maximum allowable lengths for these variable labels, they sometimes have an abbreviated form.

3. ***ICPSR reference number.*** This number is the variable number in the ICPSR edition of the codebook for the master dataset (ICPSR archive number 3131). If there is a need to refer to the original version of the question or variable for one of the items in the dataset, the ICPSR reference number will help locate that information. The variables in this module generally are simplified or condensed (and sometimes combined with adjacent filter questions) to make the analysis easier for the student. By referring to the ICPSR codebook, one can see the original items before they were processed for this dataset.

4. ***Text of question or description of variable.*** An explanation of the meaning of each variable is provided by an approximate description of the question asked or a general description of the variable. Many of the variables are relatively straightforward and need little explanation, but some types of variables require more thorough explanation and this is provided below.

   (a) There are several feeling thermometer items (V010-V011, V039-V046, V052, V054-V056), which asked the respondent to indicate his or her feeling toward a specific person or institution by placing that person or institution on a feeling thermometer that ranges from 100 to 0 degrees, where 50 degrees represents a neutral feeling, higher temperatures represent warmer or more positive feelings, and lower temperatures represent cooler or more negative feelings. Placements on the feeling thermometers have been collapsed into five categories for ease of analysis. Note that each of the major party presidential candidates has two feeling thermometer items; one asked before the election (during the September-October interviewing) and one asked after the election (in November or December).

   (b) There are a number of issue-position scales, each of which has a seven-point scale that represents possible positions that people might take on a specific issue. For example, there is an issue-position scale on government services and spending (V074), and the possible positions on the scale run from "provide many fewer services to reduce spending a lot" to "provide many more services, even if it means increased spending." Respondents were asked to place themselves on this scale according to their feelings on the issue. Only the end points of the seven-point scale are defined; respondents who feel that they fall between the two extremes can place themselves on one of the middle points. All of the issue-position scales have this basic structure.

   (c) There are other items that measure respondent orientations on public policy issues, but in a different format that the seven-point issue position scales described above. In a number of cases, a seven-point issue position scale was asked of one set of respondents and a somewhat different question on the same issue was asked of the other respondents. For example, there is a seven-point issue position scale on health care policy (V080), which runs from "having a government insurance plan that would cover all medical and hospital expenses for everyone" to "all medical expenses should be paid by individuals or private insurance plans." This question was asked of about one-half of the respondents. The remaining respondents were asked a different question (V079), which simply asked them to choose between three options: having medical expenses for everyone covered by a government plan; having medical expenses covered by individuals or private plans; or having the situation stay "the same as it is now." Although both V079 and V080 ask respondents a similar question, the difference in the response formats makes it difficult to equate a response on one item with a response on the other.

(d)   There are candidate-placement scales that indicate how the respondents felt that Bush or Gore stood on the issues. They are similar in structure to the issue-position scales to which they correspond. For example, respondents were asked where they thought Bush and Gore stood on the defense spending scale. These two candidate-placement scales (V122, V123) have seven possible categories–running from "much lower spending" to "much higher spending"-- just like the issue-position scale for defense spending (V121). The difference is that V121 measures where the respondent falls on this scale, whereas V122 and V123 measure where the respondent thinks that Bush and Gore fall on the scale. The usefulness of the candidate placement scales is that by using them in combination with the item that measures the respondent's position, one can see how closely the respondent felt he or she was to each of the two major candidates on the respective issue.

(e)   There are several indices that summarize how a respondent answered two or more questions that are related to a single topic (V014, V015, V098, V108, V132, V133, V134, V137). For example, the personal political efficacy index (V134) is based on how the respondent answered four questions dealing with feelings about one's ability to influence government. Respondents in the "high" category generally answered the questions in a very "positive" or "efficacious" manner. Respondents in the "low" category generally gave very inefficacious responses, and those in between gave mixed responses.

5.   *Value codes and value labels.* The possible values for each variable are given in the codebook. Both the numeric codes and a brief explanation of what the codes refer to are provided. If SPSS is used for the data analysis, the tables generated will have the value labels printed on them as a convenient aid (the same may be true for a number of other statistical packages). Because there are maximum allowable lengths for these labels, they often have an abbreviated form. In the sample codebook entry given above, a code of "1" indicates a vote for Bush, a code of "2" indicates a vote for Gore, and a code of "3" indicates a vote for another candidate, such as Nader. Additionally, a code of "9" is used for respondents who do not fit into any of these categories. For this last group of respondents we have only "missing data." Missing data occurs because: (a) the question does not apply to the respondent--e.g., people who did not vote were not asked which presidential candidate they voted for; (b) the respondent refused to give a response or had no opinion; or (c) the interviewer failed to obtain or record the information for some other reason. The label "NA" is attached to this category to indicate that the item

is "not applicable" or that the information was "not ascertained."

6. **Marginals**. To the left of the value descriptions and codes is a set of numbers called the marginals or marginal frequencies. The marginals indicate the total number of respondents who fall into each category of the variable. The marginals are based on the weighted data (see the discussion in Chapter III on weighting).

Interval-Level Variables

Twenty-two interval-level variables (V201 to V222) are included in this dataset in order to allow for the use of more sophisticated statistical analysis methods, such as regression analysis, that are designed for interval-level data. Unlike the previous set of variables, which are categoric in nature, these interval-level variables have a continuous set of values, running from high to low, that measure some amount or quantity. A number of these variables are the thermometer items discussed earlier, except in this case they have not been recoded into several categories. Respondents can have a score anywhere from 0 to 100 degrees on these feeling thermometers. While these thermometer items are not true interval-level variables, they are close enough to be considered such for analysis purposes. Other variables measure the number of days in the last week that the respondent used a specified media source and the respondent's age in years. There were not very many variables in the original ANES that could be considered interval level, so this set of variables is fairly limited in number and scope.

Chapter VII
Codebook

A. Voting Behavior and Related Items

V001 Voted in election (1241)

Did you vote in the elections this November?

1182	1	Voted
433	2	Did not vote
2	9	NA

V002 Presidential vote (1249)

Whom did you vote for in the presidential election? (Nonvoters are recorded as NA).

504	1	Bush
550	2	Gore
44	3	Other
456	9	NA

V003 1996 presidential vote (304)

Whom did you vote for in the 1996 presidential election? (Nonvoters are recorded as NA).

531	1	Clinton
343	2	Dole
117	3	Perot
562	9	NA

V004 House vote (1263)

Whom did you vote for in the elections for the House of Representatives? (Responses are categorized by the party of the candidate. Nonvoters are recorded as NA.)

432	1	Democrat
404	2	Republican
718	9	NA

V005 Type of House race (194)

Classification of the type of race for the House of Representatives in the respondent's congressional district. Districts were classified as to whether: (a) a Democratic incumbent was running for re-election; (b) no incumbent was running for re-election; or (c) a Republican incumbent was running for re-election. In a few cases, the respondent's congressional district was not ascertained, so these cases are coded as NA.

662	1	Democratic incumbent
154	2	Open seat
729	3	Republican incumbent
9	9	NA

V006 Senate vote (1275)

Whom did you vote for in the U. S. Senate race? (Responses are categorized by the party of the candidate. All nonvoters, including those who lived in a state that did not have a Senate election in 1996, are recorded as NA.)

394	1	Democrat
312	2	Republican
848	9	NA

V007 Type of Senate race (204)

Classification of the type of race for the U. S. Senate in the respondent's state. States were classified as to whether: (a) a Democratic incumbent was running for re-election; (b) no incumbent was running for re-election; or (c) a Republican incumbent was running for re-election. In a few cases, the respondent's state was not ascertained, so these cases are coded as NA.

429	1	Democratic incumbent
232	2	Open seat
535	3	Republican incumbent
352	4	No race in state
6	9	NA

V008 Party identification (523)

Generally speaking, do you think of yourself as a Republican, a Democrat, an independent, or what? If Democrat or Republican, would you call yourself a strong or a weak Democrat or Republican? If independent, are you closer to the Republican Party or the Democratic Party?

292	1	Strong Democrat
234	2	Weak Democrat

231	3	Independent Democrat
180	4	Independent
205	5	Independent Republican
185	6	Weak Republican
196	7	Strong Republican
30	9	NA

V009 Feeling thermometer: Democratic Party (369)

On a scale of 0 to 100 degrees, how warm or cold do you feel toward the Democratic Party?

136	1	0 - 24
232	2	25 - 49
296	3	50
474	4	51 - 75
363	5	76 - 100
53	9	NA

V010 Feeling thermometer: Republican Party (370)

On a scale of 0 to 100 degrees, how warm or cold do you feel toward the Republican Party?

147	1	0 - 24
306	2	25 - 49
311	3	50
507	4	51 - 75
230	5	76 - 100
52	9	NA

B. Political Involvement Items

V011 Interest in campaign (301, 1201)

How interested have you been in the political campaigns so far this year?

321	1	Very interested
312	2	Interested
500	3	Somewhat interested
256	4	Slightly interested
165	5	Not interested

V012 Concern over election (302)

How much would you say that you personally care who wins the election for president?

1184	1	Care a good deal
364	2	Do not care much
5	9	NA

V013 Days discussed politics last week (1204, 1205)

How many days in the past week did you talk about politics with family or friends?

640	1	6 - 7 days
352	2	3 - 5 days
222	3	1 - 2 days
318	4	0 days
22	9	NA

V014 Campaign activity index (1225-1228)

Index of respondent's activity in the campaign, built from "yes" answers to the following questions: Did you talk to any people and try to show them why they should vote for or against one of the parties or candidates?; Did you wear a campaign button, put a campaign sticker on your car, or place a sign in your window or in front of your house?; Did you go to any political meetings, rallies, speeches, dinners, or things like that in support of a particular candidate?; and Did you do any (other) work for one of the parties or candidates?

133	1	Two or more acts
475	2	One act
945	3	No acts

V015 Campaign contributions index (1229, 1231, 1233)

Index of respondent's financial contribution to the campaign, built from "yes" answers to the following questions: Did you give any money to an individual candidate running for public office? Did you give any money to a political party during this election year? and Did you give money to any other group that supported or opposed candidates?

170	1	Made contribution
1384	2	Did not contribute

C. Media Involvement Items

V016 Attention paid to presidential campaign news (1648)

How much attention did you pay to news about the campaign for President?

263	1	A great deal
393	2	Quite a bit
583	3	Some
260	4	Very little
49	5	None
5	9	NA

V017 Attention paid to congressional campaign news (1649)

How much attention did you pay to news about the congressional campaigns?

55	1	A great deal
110	2	Quite a bit
459	3	Some
651	4	Very little
274	5	None
6	9	NA

V018 Number of campaign programs watched (1202,1203)

How many television programs about the presidential campaign did you watch?

366	1	Good many
537	2	Several
357	3	One or two
291	4	None
3	9	NA

V019 Attention to national television campaign news (329,330)

How much attention did you pay to news on national news shows about the campaign for President?

187	1	A great deal
296	2	Quite a bit
450	3	Some
167	4	Very little
448	5	None
3	6	NA

V020 Attention to local campaign news (331,332,333)

How much attention did you pay to news on local news shows about the campaign for President?

161	1	A great deal
263	2	Quite a bit
485	3	Some
318	4	Very little
327	5	None

V021 Days watched national television news last week (329)

How many days in the past week did you watch the national news on TV?

443	1	6 - 7 days
345	2	3 - 5 days
328	3	1 - 2 days
432	4	0 days
6	9	NA

V022   Days watched local television early news last week (331)

How many days in the past week did you watch the local early TV news?

463	1	6 - 7 days
349	2	3 - 5 days
249	3	1 - 2 days
493	4	0 days

V023 Days watched local television late news last week (332)

How many days in the past week did you watch the local late TV news?

330	1	6 - 7 days
340	2	3 - 5 days
279	3	1 - 2 days
603	4	0 days
1	9	NA

V024 Watched presidential debate? (1644,1645)

Did you watch any of the televised presidential debates between George Bush and Al Gore?

413	1	Watched entire debate
623	2	Watched part of debate

```
509   3   Did not watch debate
  8   9   NA
```

V025 Days read newspaper last week (335)

How many days in the past week did you read a daily newspaper?

```
513   1   7 days
282   2   3-6 days
338   3   1-2 days
420   4   0 days
```

V026 Attention paid to campaign news in newspapers (335,336,337)

How much attention did you pay to newspaper articles about the campaign for president?

```
 93   1   Great deal
164   2   Quite a bit
294   3   Some
 86   4   Very little
914   5   None
  1   9   NA
```

V027 Number of campaign speeches heard on radio (1646,1647)

How many speeches or discussions about the campaign on the radio would you say you listened to?

```
122   1   Good many
221   2   Several
236   3   One or two
970   4   None
  5   9   NA
```

V028 Listen to talk radio? (1431)

How much attention do you pay to political talk radio programs in which people call in to voice their opinions about politics?

```
 158   1   Most days
 141   2   1 - 2 days per week
 237   3   Occasionally
1018   4   Not at all
```

V029 Viewed election information on Internet? (1433,1434)

Do you view information on the internet as a source to find out about presidential elections?

435	1	Yes
1119	2	No

V030 Trust in media (1429)

How much of the time do you think you can trust the media to report the news fairly?

114	1	Almost always
640	2	Most of the time
670	3	Some of the time
128	4	Almost never
2	9	NA

D. Candidate Image Items

V031 Gore: really cares? (525)

How well does the phrase "he really cares about people like you" describe Al Gore?

822	1	Quite well
625	2	Not very well
107	9	NA

V032 Gore: knowledgeable? (526)

How well does the phrase "he is knowledgeable" describe Al Gore?

1228	1	Quite well
255	2	Not very well
71	9	NA

V033 Gore: strong leader? (527)

How well does the phrase "he presents strong leadership" describe Al Gore?

843	1	Quite well
613	2	Not very well
98	9	NA

V034 Gore: dishonest? (528)

How well does the phrase "he is dishonest" describe Al Gore?

398	1	Quite well
1003	2	Not very well
152	9	NA

V035 Bush: really cares? (532)

How well does the phrase "he really cares about people like you" describe George Bush?

674	1	Quite well
761	2	Not very well
118	9	NA

V036 Bush: knowledgeable? (533)

How well does the phrase "he is knowledgeable" describe George Bush?

1056	1	Quite well
416	2	Not very well
82	9	NA

V037 Bush: strong leader? (534)

How well does the phrase "he provides strong leadership" describe George Bush?

960	1	Quite well
479	2	Not very well
115	9	NA

V038 Bush: dishonest? (535)

How well does the phrase "he is dishonest" describe George Bush?

287	1	Quite well
1070	2	Not very well
197	9	NA

V039 Gore: pre-election feeling thermometer (360)

On a scale of 0 degrees to 100 degrees, how warm or cool do you feel towards Al Gore? (assessed before the election)

169	1	0 - 24
260	2	25 - 49

243	3	50
501	4	51 - 75
353	5	76-100
28	9	NA

V040 Gore: post-election feeling thermometer (1293)

On a scale of 0 degrees to 100 degrees, how warm or cool do you feel towards Al Gore? (assessed after the election)

246	1	0 - 24
280	2	25 - 49
192	3	50
470	4	51 - 75
349	5	76-100
18	9	NA

V041 Bush: pre-election feeling thermometer (361)

On a scale of 0 degrees to 100 degrees, how warm or cool do you feel towards George Bush? (assessed before the election)

137	1	0 - 24
287	2	25 - 49
292	3	50
473	4	51 - 75
329	5	76-100
36	9	NA

V042 Bush: post-election feeling thermometer (1294)

On a scale of 0 degrees to 100 degrees, how warm or cool do you feel towards George Bush? (assessed after the election)

183	1	0 - 24
322	2	25 - 49
218	3	50
421	4	51 - 75
396	5	76-100
14	9	NA

V043 Nader: feeling thermometer (363)

On a scale of 0 degrees to 100 degrees, how warm or cool do you feel towards Ralph Nader? (assessed before the election)

| 126 | 1 | 0 - 24 |
| 175 | 2 | 25 - 49 |

344	3	50
312	4	51 - 75
142	5	76-100
455	9	NA

V044 Buchanan: feeling thermometer (362)

On a scale of 0 degrees to 100 degrees, how warm or cool do you feel towards Pat Buchanan? (assessed before the election)

283	1	0 - 24
279	2	25 - 49
414	3	50
234	4	51 - 75
46	5	76-100
298	9	NA

V045 Lieberman: feeling thermometer (366)

On a scale of 0 degrees to 100 degrees, how warm or cool do you feel towards Joseph Lieberman? (assessed before the election)

96	1	0 - 24
153	2	25 - 49
325	3	50
348	4	51 - 75
185	5	76-100
447	9	NA

V046 Cheney: feeling thermometer (367)

On a scale of 0 degrees to 100 degrees, how warm or cool do you feel towards Richard Cheney? (assessed before the election)

81	1	0 - 24
135	2	25 - 49
350	3	50
386	4	51 - 75
197	5	76-100
405	9	NA

E. Presidential approval and government performance item

V047 Clinton job approval (341)

Do you approve or disapprove of the way that Bill Clinton is handling his job as president?

625	1	S trongly approve
355	2	Approve
140	3	Disapprove
371	4	Strongly disapprove
63	9	NA

V048 Clinton: moral? (1637a)

How well does the phrase "he is moral" describe Bill Clinton?

252	1	Quite well
1270	2	Not very well
32	9	NA

V049 Clinton: cares? (1638a)

How well does the phrase "he really cares about people like you" describe Bill Clinton?

764	1	Quite well
753	2	Not very well
37	9	NA

V050 Clinton: strong leader? (1640a)

How well does the phrase "he presents strong leadership" describe Bill Clinton?

995	1	Quite well
537	2	Not very well
22	9	NA

V051 Clinton: dishonest? (1641a)

How well does the phrase "he is dishonest" describe Bill Clinton?

930	1	Quite well
582	2	Not very well
42	9	NA

V052 Clinton: feeling thermometer (359)

On a scale of 0 degrees to 100 degrees, how warm or cool do you feel towards Bill Clinton?

265	1	0-24
247	2	25-49
186	3	50
430	4	51-75
416	5	76-100
10	9	NA

V053 Approval of Congress (358)

Do you approve or disapprove of the way the that the U.S. Congress is handling its job?

250	1	Strongly approve
558	2	Approve
257	3	Disapprove
260	4	Strongly disapprove
229	9	NA

V054 Congress: feeling thermometer (1305)

On a scale of 0 degrees to 100 degrees, how warm or cool do you feel towards Congress (assessed after the election)?

53	1	0-24
221	2	25-49
392	3	50
631	4	51-75
184	5	76-100
73	9	NA

V055 Supreme Court: feeling thermometer (1304)

On a scale of 0 degrees to 100 degrees, how warm or cool do you feel towards the Supreme Court?

38	1	0-24
101	2	25-49
326	3	50
619	4	51-75
391	5	76-100
79	9	NA

V056 Federal government: feeling thermometer (1307)

On a scale of 0 degrees to 100 degrees, how warm or cool do you feel towards the Federal government?

107	1	0-24
288	2	25-49
329	3	50
574	4	51-75
188	5	76-100
68	9	NA

V057 Most important problem for US (436)

What do you think is the most important problem facing this country? (NOTE: This question was only asked of one-half of the full sample.)

111	1	Economy and government spending
114	2	Education
131	3	Health care and social welfare
75	4	Social Security and Medicare
83	5	Moral problems
87	6	Crime
67	7	Other domestic problems
85	8	Foreign affairs and defense
800	9	NA

V058 Government performance on most important problem (437)

How good a job is the government in Washington doing in dealing with this problem? (NOTE: This question was asked of only asked of one-half of the full sample.)

73	1	Good
317	2	Fair
345	3	Poor
819	9	NA

V059 Party performance on most important problem (438)

Which political party do you think would be most likely to get the government to do a better job in dealing with this problem? (NOTE: This question was asked of only one-half of the full sample.)

170	1	Republicans better
365	2	No difference
197	3	Democrats better
822	9	NA

F. Economic conditions items

V060 Better or worse off financially? (1412a)

Would you say that you were better off or worse off financially than you were last year?

157	1	Much better
357	2	Somewhat better
838	3	About the same
144	4	Somewhat worse
51	5	Much worse
7	9	NA

V061 Better or worse off next year? (1417a)

Do you think that a year from now you will be better or worse off financially?

196	1	Much better
385	2	Somewhat better
847	3	About the same
66	4	Somewhat worse
24	5	Much worse
35	9	NA

V062 Economy since 1992 (1599a)

Would you say that since 1992 the nation's economy has gotten better, stayed about the same, or gotten worse?

565	1	Much better
496	2	Somewhat better
368	3	About the same
61	4	Somewhat worse
31	5	Much worse
32	9	NA

V063 Economy last year (491)

Would you say that over the past year the nation's economy has gotten better, stayed about the same, or gotten worse?

207	1	Much better
375	2	Somewhat better
690	3	About the same
63	4	Somewhat worse

| 204 | 5 | Much worse |
| 14 | 9 | NA |

V064 Economy next year (499)

What about the next 12 months? Do you expect the economy to get better, get worse or stay about the same?

104	1	Much better
252	2	Somewhat better
865	3	About the same
215	4	Somewhat worse
61	5	Much worse
57	9	NA

V065 Clinton effect on economy (1603a)

Would you say that Bill Clinton has made the nation's economy better, made it worse, or had no effect on the economy?

379	1	Much better
471	2	Somewhat better
594	3	No effect
38	4	Somewhat worse
19	5	Much worse
54	9	NA

V066 Clinton handling of economy (503)

Do you approve or disapprove of the way that Bill Clinton is handling the economy?

650	1	Strongly approve
442	2	Approve
134	3	Disapprove
226	4	Strongly disapprove
102	9	NA

V067 Best party for economy (505)

Which political party do you think would be most likely to get the government to do a better job in dealing with this problem?

430	1	Democrats better
717	2	No difference
359	3	Republicans better
48	9	NA

G. Ideology items

V068 Ideology (1368)

Respondent's self-placement on a scale running from "liberal" to "conservative."

196	1	Liberal
128	2	Slightly liberal
375	3	Moderate
180	4	Slightly conservative
296	5	Conservative
378	9	NA

V069 Gore: ideological placement (1372)

Respondent's placement of Al Gore on a scale running from "liberal" to "conservative."

635	1	Liberal
271	2	Slightly liberal
206	3	Moderate
100	4	Slightly conservative
146	5	Conservative
195	9	NA

V070 Bush: ideological placement (1374)

Respondent's placement of George Bush on a scale running from "liberal" to "conservative."

128	1	Liberal
81	2	Slightly liberal
173	3	Moderate
255	4	Slightly conservative
714	5	Conservative
202	9	NA

V071 Democratic Party: ideological placement (1382)

Respondent's placement of the Democratic Party on a scale running from "liberal" to "conservative."

657	1	Liberal
281	2	Slightly liberal
210	3	Moderate
65	4	Slightly conservative
128	5	Conservative
211	9	NA

V072 Republican Party: ideological placement (1383)

Respondent's placement of the Republican Party on a scale running from "liberal" to "conservative."

118	1	Liberal
73	2	Slightly liberal
167	3	Moderate
250	4	Slightly conservative
724	5	Conservative
222	9	NA

H. Social welfare and domestic spending issue items

V073 Government services: increase or decrease? (1386)

Do you that the government should provide fewer services in order to reduce spending or should it increase the services it provides even if it means increasing spending? (NOTE: This question was only asked of one-half of the full sample.)

152	1	Reduce services and spending
347	2	Stay the same
294	3	Increase services and spending
761	9	NA

V074 Government services scale (1385)

Respondent's self-placement on a scale running from "Government should provide many fewer services to reduce spending a lot" to "Government should provide many more services, even if it means increasing spending." (NOTE: This question was only asked of one-half of the full sample.)

19	1	Many fewer services
55	2	
96	3	
174	4	
153	5	
45	6	
44	7	Many more services
968	9	NA

V075 Jobs and living standards: government vs. individual (616)

Should the government in Washington see to it that every person has a job and a good standard of living or should the government just let people get ahead on their own? (NOTE: This question was only asked of one-half of the full sample.)

166	1	Government should see to it
41	2	Depends
405	3	Leave people on own
942	9	NA

V076 Jobs and living standards scale (615)

Respondent's self placement on a scale running from "Government should see to it that every person has a job and a good standard of living" to "Government should let each person get ahead on their own." (NOTE: This question was only asked of one-half of the full sample.)

67	1	Government should guarantee
41	2	
84	3	
144	4	
153	5	
154	6	
109	7	Individual on own
802	9	NA

V077 Gore: jobs and living standards scale position (621)

Respondent's placement of Al Gore on a scale running from "Government should see to it that every person has a job and a good standard of living" to "Government should let each person get ahead on their own." (NOTE: This question was only asked of one-half of the full sample.)

64	1	Government should guarantee
94	2	
172	3	
180	4	
87	5	
52	6	
40	7	Individual on own
865	9	NA

V078 Bush: jobs and living standards scale position (626)

Respondent' placement of George Bush on a scale running from "Government should see to it that every person has a job and a good standard of living" to "Government should let each person get ahead on their own." (NOTE: This question was only asked of one-half of the full sample.)

23	1	Government should guarantee
22	2	

72	3	
154	4	
166	5	
167	6	
78	7	Individual on own
871	9	NA

V079 Health insurance: government vs. private plans (611)

Should there be a government insurance plan that would cover all medical and hospital expenses for everyone, or should medical expenses should be paid by individuals or by private insurance plans." (NOTE: This question was only asked of one-half of the full sample.)

310	1	Government health plan
43	2	Same as now
257	3	Private health plans
944	9	NA

V080 Government health insurance scale (609)

Respondent's placement on a scale that runs from "There should be a government insurance plan which would cover all medical and hospital expenses for everyone" to "All medical expenses should be paid by individuals or by private insurance plans."   (NOTE: This question was only asked of one-half of the full sample.)

130	1	Government plan
82	2	
122	3	
162	4	
115	5	
80	6	
85	7	Private plans
778	9	NA

V081 Spending on welfare programs (676)

Should federal spending on welfare programs be increased, decreased, or kept the same?

262	1	Increase
690	2	About the same
577	3	Decrease
24	9	NA

V082 Spending on aid for the poor (680)

Should federal spending on programs to aid the poor be increased, decreased, or kept the same?

820	1	Increase
571	2	About the same
134	3	Decrease
29	9	NA

V083 Spending on Social Security (681)

Should federal spending on social security be increased, decreased, or kept the same?

977	1	Increase
483	2	About the same
63	3	Decrease
31	9	NA

V084 Spending on public schools (683)

Should federal spending on education be increased, decreased, or kept the same?

1178	1	Increase
284	2	About the same
83	3	Decrease
8	9	NA

V085 Use budget surplus for Social Security? (693)

Do you approve or disapprove of the proposal to use most of the expected federal budget surplus to protect social security and Medicare?

999	1	Strongly approve
267	2	Approve
124	3	Disapprove
132	4	Strongly disapprove
32	9	NA

V086 Use budget surplus for tax cuts? (690)

Do you approve or disapprove of the proposal to use most of the expected federal budget surplus to cut taxes?

736	1	Strongly approve
260	2	Approve

190	3	Disapprove
315	4	Strongly disapprove
53	9	NA

I. Social issue items

V087 Abortion (694)

Respondent's agreement with one of the following statements: (1) By law, abortion should never be permitted; (2) The law should permit abortion only in case of rape, incest, or when the woman's life is in danger; (3) The law should permit abortion for reasons other than rape, incest, or danger to the woman's life, but only after the need for the abortion has been clearly established; (4) By law, a woman should always be able to obtain an abortion as a matter of personal choice.

202	1	Never permitted
479	2	For rape and incest only
236	3	If clear need
598	4	Always permitted
39	9	NA

V088 Gore: abortion position (696)

Respondent's placement of Al Gore on the abortion scale.

77	1	Never permitted
217	2	For rape and incest only
220	3	If clear need
620	4	Always permitted
420	9	NA

V089 Bush: abortion position (698)

Respondent's placement of George Bush on the abortion scale.

243	1	Never permitted
545	2	For rape and incest only
195	3	If clear need
111	4	Always permitted
459	9	NA

V090 Gun control (731)

Do you think that the federal government should make it easier or more difficult for individuals to buy a gun?

905	1	More difficult
580	2	Same as now
58	3	Easier
11	9	NA

V091 Gore: gun control position (735)

Respondent's perception of where Al Gore stands on the question of gun control (see V090).

939	1	More difficult
321	2	Same as now
15	3	Easier
278	9	NA

V092   Bush: gun control position (739)

Respondent's perception of where George Bush stands on the question of gun control (see V090)

322	1	More difficult
693	2	Same as now
248	3	Easier
291	9	NA

V093   Best way to reduce crime (1482a)

Respondent's self-placement on a scale running from "The best way to reduce crime is to address the social problems that cause crime, like bad schools, poverty and joblessness" to "The best way to reduce crime is to make sure that criminals are caught, convicted and punished."   (NOTE: This question was only asked of one-half of the full sample.)

335	1	Address social problems
262	2	Depends
222	3	Better to punish criminals
735	9	NA

V094 Crime prevention scale (1482)

(NOTE: This question was only asked of one-half of the full sample.)

75	1	Address social problems
61	2	
69	3	
136	4	
82	5	
62	6	

| 147 | 7 | Vigorously enforce laws |
| 922 | 9 | NA |

V095 Death penalty (752)

Do you favor or oppose the death penalty for persons convicted of murder?

815	1	Strongly favor
279	2	Favor
141	3	Oppose
239	4	Strongly oppose
80	9	NA

V096 School vouchers (742)

Do you favor or oppose a program that would allow parents to use tax funds to send their children to the school of their choice, even if it were a private school?

647	1	Favor
535	2	Oppose
371	9	NA

V097 Desirable immigration level (510)

Do you think that the number of immigrants from foreign countries who are permitted to come the U.S. to live should be increased, decreased, or kept the same?

125	1	Increased
667	2	Same level
701	3	Decreased
61	9	NA

V098 Lifestyle tolerance index (computed from 1530-1533)

Index of respondent's tolerance to alternative lifestyles built from agreement or disagreement with the following statements: The world is always changing and we should adjust our view of moral behavior to those changes; We should be more tolerant of people who choose to live according to their own moral standards even if they are very different from our own; This country would have many fewer problems if there were more emphasis on traditional family ties; and The newer lifestyles are contributing to the breakdown of our society. (NOTE: Scores on this index are relative; individuals

237	1	High tolerance
369	2	
334	3	
394	4	

195	5	Low tolerance
24	9	NA

J. Civil rights and equality issue items

V099 Government aid to blacks (642)

Do you think that the federal government should make every effort to improve the social and economic position of blacks, or should the government should not make any special effort to help blacks because they should help themselves. (NOTE: This question was only asked of one-half of the full sample.)

173	1	Government should help
82	2	Depends
300	3	No special help
998	9	NA

V100 Minority aid scale (641)

Respondent's self-placement on a scale running from "Government should make every effort to improve the social and economic position of blacks" to "Government should not make any special effort to help blacks because they should help themselves." (NOTE: This question was only asked of one-half of the full sample.)

48	1	Government should help greatly
35	2	
64	3	
210	4	
123	5	
128	6	
165	7	No special help at all
780	9	NA

V101 Gore: minority aid scale position (651)

Respondent's placement of Al Gore on a scale running from "Government should make every effort to improve the social and economic position of blacks" to "Government should not make any special effort to help blacks because they should help themselves." (NOTE: This question was only asked of one-half of the full sample.)

80	1	Government should help greatly
110	2	
153	3	
178	4	

64	5	
54	6	
24	7	No special help at all
891	9	NA

V102 Bush: minority aid scale position (656)

Respondent's placement of George Bush on a scale running from "Government should make every effort to improve the social and economic position of blacks" to "Government should not make any special effort to help blacks because they should help themselves." (NOTE: This question was only asked of one-half of the full sample.)

17	1	Government should help greatly
25	2	
67	3	
175	4	
179	5	
104	6	
86	7	No special help at all
900	9	NA

V103 Job preferences for blacks (806)

Do you favor or oppose preferential hiring and promotion of blacks because of past discrimination?

146	1	Strongly favor
82	2	Favor
323	3	Oppose
856	4	Strongly oppose
147	9	NA

V104 Affirmative action programs (674a)

Do you think that a company that has discriminated against blacks should be required to have an affirmative action program?

537	1	Strongly favor
201	2	Favor
164	3	Oppose
467	4	Strongly oppose
185	9	NA

V105 Government help for blacks needed? (computed from 1508-1511)

Index computed from the respondent's agreement or disagreement with the following statements: Blacks should work their way up without special favors, just as other minorities did; Over the past few years, blacks have gotten less than they deserve; If blacks would only try harder, they could be just as well off as whites; and Generations of slavery and discrimination have created conditions that make it difficult for blacks to work their way our of the lower class.

298	1	Need help
277	2	
404	3	
253	4	
278	5	Do not need help
44	9	NA

V106 Job protection for gays (1481)

Do you favor or oppose laws to protect homosexuals against job discrimination?

585	1	Strongly favor
398	2	Favor
211	3	Oppose
276	4	Strongly oppose
84	9	NA

V107 Gays in the military (727)

Do you favor or oppose allowing homosexuals to serve in the United States Armed Forces?

758	1	Strongly favor
347	2	Favor
69	3	Oppose
287	4	Strongly oppose
93	9	NA

V108 Equality index (computed from 1521-1526)

Index of respondent's commitment to equality built from agreement or disagreement with the following statements: Our society should do whatever necessary to make sure that everyone has an equal opportunity to succeed; This country would be better off if we worried less about how equal people are; It is not really that big a problem if some people have more of a chance in life than others; If people were treated more equally in this country we would have many fewer problems; and One of the big problems in this country is we don't give everyone an equal chance. (NOTE: Scores on this index are relative; individuals classified as "high" (or "low") are simply higher (lower) than others not high (low) in an absolute sense.

322	1	High emphasis
432	2	
246	3	

300	4	
223	5	Low emphasis
32	9	NA

K. Environmental issue items

V109 Spending on environmental protection (682)

Should federal spending on the environment be increased, decreased, or remain the same?

773	1	Increase
604	2	About the same
145	3	Decrease
31	9	NA

V110 Protect environment or jobs? (710)

Do you think that it is more important to protect the environment even if it costs jobs or reduces our standard of living, or is it more important to protect jobs and the standard of living? (NOTE: This question was only asked of one-half of the full sample.)

363	1	Protect environment
66	2	Depends
141	3	Protect jobs
983	9	NA

V111 Environmental protection scale (708)

Respondent's self-placement on a scale running from "It is important to protect the environment even if it costs some jobs or otherwise reduces our standard of living" to "Protecting the environment is not as important as maintaining jobs and our standard of living." (NOTE: This question was only asked of one-half of the full sample.)

95	1	Strongly protect environment
97	2	
127	3	
241	4	
115	5	
53	6	
37	7	Strongly protect jobs
788	9	NA

V112　Gore: environmental protection scale position (714)

Respondent's placement of Al Gore on a scale running from "It is important to protect the environment even if it costs some jobs or otherwise reduces our standard of living" to "Protecting the environment is not as important as maintaining jobs and our standard of living." (NOTE: This question was only asked of one-half of the full sample.)

109	1	Strongly protect environment
122	2	
135	3	
156	4	
72	5	
37	6	
23	7	Strongly protect jobs
900	9	NA

V113　Bush: environmental protection scale position (719)

Respondent's placement of George Bush on a scale running from "It is important to protect the environment even if it costs some jobs or otherwise reduces our standard of living" to "Protecting the environment is not as important as maintaining jobs and our standard of living." (NOTE: This question was only asked of one-half of the full sample.)

23	1	Strongly protect environment
18	2	
64	3	
175	4	
165	5	
125	6	
45	7	Strongly protect jobs
937	9	NA

V114　More or less environmental regulation needed? (772)

Do you think that we need much tougher environmental regulations on business to protect the environment, or are the existing regulations already too much of a burden on business? (NOTE: This question was only asked of one-half of the full sample.)

298	1	Tougher regulations needed
59	2	Depends
111	3	Regulations already too tough
1085	9	NA

V115 Environmental regulation scale (771)

Respondent's self placement on a scale running from "We need much tougher environmental regulations on business to protect the environment" to "Existing environmental regulations are already too much of a burden on business." (NOTE: This question was only asked of one-half of the full sample.)

143	1	Much tougher regulation
114	2	
117	3	
149	4	
64	5	
42	6	
29	7	Regulations too tough
894	9	NA

V116 Gore: environmental regulation scale position (778)

Respondent's placement of Al Gore on a scale running from "We need much tougher environmental regulations on business to protect the environment" to "Existing environmental regulations are already too much of a burden on business." (NOTE: This question was only asked of one-half of the full sample.)

128	1	Much tougher regulation
171	2	
141	3	
129	4	
42	5	
22	6	
10	7	Regulations too tough
911	9	NA

V117 Bush: environmental regulation scale position (785)

Respondent's placement of George Bush on a scale running from "We need much tougher environmental regulations on business to protect the environment" to "Existing environmental regulations are already too much of a burden on business." (NOTE: This question was only asked of one-half of the full sample.)

22	1	Much tougher regulation
39	2	
87	3	
176	4	
141	5	
107	6	

48	7	Regulations too tough
934	9	NA

L. Foreign affairs and defense issue items

V118 US position in world (507)

During the past year, has the U.S. position in the world grown stronger, stayed about the same, or become weaker?

419	1	Weaker
756	2	About the same
352	3	Stronger
26	9	NA

V119 US world role (514)

Do you think that this country would be better off if we just stayed home and did not concern ourselves with problems in other parts of the world, or would we be better off if we tried to solve problems in other parts of the world?

453	1	Better off to stay home
1045	2	Better off solving problems
55	9	NA

V120 More or less defense spending? (583)

Do you think that defense spending should be increased, decreased, or kept the same? (NOTE: This question was only asked of one-half of the full sample.)

90	1	Decrease spending
123	2	Keep the same
284	3	Increase spending
1056	9	NA

V121 Defense spending scale (581)

Respondent's self-placement on a scale running from "We should spend much less on defense" to "We should greatly increase defense spending." (NOTE: This question was only asked of one-half of the full sample.)

30	1	Much lower spending
29	2	
58	3	
181	4	
185	5	

126	6	
77	7	Much higher spending
867	9	NA

V122 Gore: defense spending scale position (588)

Respondent's placement of Al Gore on a scale running from "We should spend much less on defense" to "We should greatly increase defense spending." (NOTE: This question was only asked of one-half of the full sample.)

23	1	Much lower spending
66	2	
127	3	
203	4	
165	5	
64	6	
29	7	Much higher spending
876	9	NA

V123 Bush: defense spending scale position (593)

Respondent's placement of George Bush on a scale running from "We should spend much less on defense" to "We should greatly increase defense spending." (NOTE: This question was only asked of one-half of the full sample.)

9	1	Much lower spending
20	2	
51	3	
145	4	
211	5	
170	6	
87	7	Much higher spending
861	9	NA

V124 Spending on foreign aid (678)

Should federal spending on foreign aid be increased, decreased, or kept the same?

138	1	Increase
674	2	About the same
700	3	Decrease
42	9	NA

V125 US more secure? (1608a)

Would you say that compared to 1992, the U.S. is more secure from its foreign enemies, less secure, or has there not been much change?

376	1	More secure
699	2	No change
424	3	Less secure
55	9	NA

V126 Clinton effect on US security (1612a)

Would you say that the Clinton administration has made the U.S. more secure from its foreign enemies, less secure, or has there not been much change?

350	1	Made more secure
783	2	No effect
362	3	Made less secure
59	9	NA

V127 Best party to avoid war (506)

Do you think that the problem of keeping the U.S. out of war would be better handled during the next four years by the Democrats, the Republicans, or about the same by both parties?

302	1	Democrats
951	2	No difference
262	3	Republicans
38	9	NA

M. General government orientation items

V128 Trust government to do right? (V001534)

How much of the time do you think you can trust the government in Washington to do what is right?

866	1	Some or none of time
676	2	All or most of time
12	9	NA

V129 How much tax waste? (V001535)

Do you think that people in government waste a lot of the money we pay in taxes, waste some of it, or don't waste very much of it?

906	1	A lot of waste
633	2	Not a lot
15	9	NA

V130 Government run for all? (V001536)

Would you say the government is pretty much run by a few big interests looking out for themselves or that it is run for the benefit of all the people?

934	1	For a few
532	2	For all
87	9	NA

V131 Government officials crooked? (V001537)

Do you think that quite a few of the people running the government are crooked or that not very many of them are?

568	1	Quite a few
952	2	Not many
34	9	NA

V132 Trust in government index (computed from V001534-V001537)

Index of respondent's trust in government built from answers to statements in V128, V129, V130, and V131.

301	1	Low
334	2	
325	3	
287	4	
202	5	High
104	9	NA

V133 Big government index (computed from V001420-V001422)

Index of respondent's attitude towards size of government built from selections from the following pairs of statements: (1) The less government the better, versus There are more things government should be doing; (2) We need a strong government to handle today's complex economic problems, versus The free market can handle these problems without government being involved; and (3) The main reason government has become bigger over the years is because it has gotten involved in things that people should do for themselves, versus Government has become bigger because the problems we face have become bigger.

321	1	Low support
247	2	
322	3	
586	4	High support
78	9	NA

V134 Personal political efficacy index (computed from V001516-V001519)

Index of respondent's feelings of personal political efficacy built from agreement or disagreement with the following statements: I have a pretty good understanding of important political issues facing the country; I consider myself well-qualified to participate in politics; I fell that I could do as good a job in public office as most other people; I think that I am better informed about politics and government than most people.

171	1	High
328	2	
390	3	
364	4	
280	5	Low
20	9	NA

V135 Public officials do not care? (V001527)

Do you agree or disagree with the statement, "I don't think public officials care much what people like me think?"

294	1	Agree strongly
587	2	Agree somewhat
163	3	Neither agree nor disagree
414	4	Disagree somewhat
85	5	Disagree strongly
11	9	NA

V136 People have no say? (V001528)

Do you agree or disagree with the statement, "People like me don't have any say about what the government does?"

240	1	Agree strongly
395	2	Agree somewhat
147	3	Neither agree nor disagree
571	4	Disagree somewhat
191	5	Disagree strongly
10	9	NA

V137 Institutional political efficacy index (computed from V001527, V001528)

Index of institutional political efficacy, constructed from responses to V135 and V136.

147	1	High
398	2	
318	3	
411	4	
268	5	Low
13	9	NA

V138 Politics too complicated? (V001529)

Do you agree or disagree with the statement, "Sometimes politics and government seem so complicated that a person like me can't really understand what's going on?"

355	1	Agree strongly
583	2	Agree somewhat
114	3	Neither agree nor disagree
314	4	Disagree somewhat
183	5	Disagree strongly
6	9	NA

V139 Satisfaction with US democracy (V001651)

Are you satisfied or dissatisfied with the way that democracy works in the U.S.?

447	1	Satisfied
683	2	Fairly satisfied
279	3	Not very satisfied
144	9	NA

V140 Favor two-party system? (V001650)

Which of the following would you prefer to see?: (1) A continuation of the two party system of Democrats and Republicans; (2) Elections in which candidates run as individuals without party labels; or (3) The growth of one or more parties that could effectively challenge the Democrats and Republicans?

565	1	Keep two parties
436	2	Nonpartisan system
494	3	New parties
59	9	NA

V141 Favor divided government? (V000397)

Do you think that it is better when one party controls both the presidency and Congress, better when control is divided, or doesn't it matter?

360	1	Control by one party
380	2	Does not matter
783	3	Divided government
31	9	NA

V142 Campaign finance reform (V001489)

Is it more important to protect government from excessive influence by campaign contributors, or is it more important to protect the freedom of individuals to financially support political candidates and parties?

656	1	Protect against undue influence
225	2	Protect freedom to contribute
672	9	NA

V143 Fairness of election (V001291)

Do you believe that the November election was fair or unfair

303	1	Very fair
420	2	Somewhat unfair
165	3	Neither fair nor unfair
321	4	Somewhat unfair
213	5	Very unfair
131	9	NA

N. Demographic items

V144 Gender (1029)

Respondent's gender.

670	1	Male
884	2	Female

V145 Race (1006a, 1012)

Respondent's race or ethnicity.

1172	1	White, non-Hispanic
181	2	Black
111	3	Hispanic

80	4	Other
10	9	NA

V146 Age (908)

Respondent's age.

199	1	18-24
264	2	25-34
359	3	35-44
260	4	45-54
201	5	55-64
265	6	65 & older
6	9	NA

V147 Marital status (909)

Respondent's marital status.

889	1	Married
368	2	Single
180	3	Divorced, Separated
108	4	Widowed
9	9	NA

V148 Children (1023, 1024)

Respondent's children.

563	1	Children under 18
572	2	Adult children only
414	3	No children
4	9	NA

V149 Education (913)

What is the highest grade of school you have completed?

231	1	Less than HS
516	2	HS graduate
310	3	Some college, no degree
125	4	Some college, AA degree
244	5	College degree
122	6	Advanced degree
6	9	NA

V150 Income (994)

What was the total income for your family last year?

179	1	Less than $15k
328	2	$15k to $35k
388	3	$35k to $65k
181	4	$65k to $85k
218	5	$85k and over
259	9	NA

V151 Social class (1005)

Do you think of yourself as working class or middle class?

716	1	Working class
579	2	Middle class
189	3	Upper middle class
69	9	NA

V152 Employment status (920)

Are you employed, looking for work, retired, or what?

962	1	Employed
78	2	Unemployed
321	3	Retired, disabled
136	4	Homemaker
53	5	Student
3	9	NA

V153 Occupation (979)

What is your primary occupation? (Retired, disabled, and unemployed individuals are classified according to their previous employment.)

443	1	Professional/managerial
197	2	Technical/clerical
366	3	Sales/service
274	4	Skilled manual
78	5	Unskilled manual
26	6	Farming/fishing
171	9	NA

V154 Union membership (990)

Does anyone in your household belong to a labor union?

242	1	Yes
1303	2	No
8	9	NA

V155 Religious affiliation (904)

What is your religious preference or affiliation? (Note: Mainline protestants include Episcopalians, Lutherans, Methodists, Presbyterians, and other smaller sects; Evangelical protestants include Baptists, Pentecostal churches, and other smaller churches; Catholic includes Roman Catholics and Eastern Orthodox churches; Other includes mostly Mormons, Jehovah's Witnesses, Christian Scientists, and Muslims.)

409	1	Mainline Protestant
388	2	Evangelical Protestant
422	3	Catholic
31	4	Jewish
65	5	Other
216	6	None
22	9	NA

V156 Importance of religion (872, 873)

Index of importance of religion to the respondent built from the following questions: "Do you consider religion to be an important part of your life, or not?" and "How much guidance would you say religion plays in your day-to-day living?"

586	1	Great deal
329	2	Quite a bit
262	3	Some
372	4	None
5	9	NA

V157 Church attendance (877, 879)

How often do you go to religious services?

396	1	Every week
403	2	Few times a month
232	3	Few times a year
512	4	Never
12	9	NA

V158 Region (79)

Region of the country that the respondent lives in.

328	1	Northeast
380	2	Midwest
518	3	South
322	4	West
6	9	NA

V159 Size of community (93)

Size of community the respondent lives in. (Note: Large urban areas are the 21 largest Metropolitan Statistical Areas, and medium urban areas are all other MSAs. Respondents not living in an MSA are classified as living in a town or rural area.)

219	1	Large urban area
379	2	Medium-sized urban area
247	3	Town or rural area
6	9	NA

V160 Type of place (93)

Type of community the respondent lives in. (Note: Central cities are defined as the central cities of Metropolitan statistical areas. Suburban areas are defined as the remaining portions of the MSAs. Respondents not living in an MSA are classified as living in a town or rural area.)

236	1	Central city
362	2	Suburb
247	3	Town or rural area
709	9	NA

O. Interval-level Variables for Further Analysis

The following variables are interval-level, or close to interval-level, measures that can be employed in statistical analyses where categoric data would be inappropriate, such as regression analysis. These variables are included for the convenience of those who want to go beyond the basic crosstabulation methods described in this manual.

The media variables are expressed in number of days per week of exposure (missing data are coded as 9). The thermometer items are expressed in actual degrees, running from 0 degrees to 100 degrees (missing data are coded as 999). Age is expressed in years (missing data are coded as 99).

V201 Days watched national news last week (329)

How many days in the past week did you watch the national news on TV?

V202 Days watched local early news last week (331)

How many days in the past week did you watch the local early TV news?

V203 Days watched local late news last week (332)

How many days in the past week did you watch the local late TV news?

V204 Days read newspaper last week (335)

How many days in the past week did you read a daily newspaper?

V205 Gore: pre-election feeling thermometer (360)

On a scale of 0 to 100 degrees, how warm or cool do you feel toward Al Gore? (assessed before the election)

V206 Gore: post-election feeling thermometer (1293)

On a scale of 0 to 100 degrees, how warm or cool do you feel toward Al Gore? (assessed after the election)

V207 Bush: pre-election feeling thermometer (361)

On a scale of 0 to 100 degrees, how warm or cool do you feel toward George W. Bush? (assessed before the election)

V208 Bush: post-election feeling thermometer (1294)

On a scale of 0 to 100 degrees, how warm or cool do you feel toward George W. Bush? (assessed after the election)

V209 Nader: feeling thermometer (363)

On a scale of 0 to 100 degrees, how warm or cool do you feel toward Ralph Nader? (assessed before the election)

V210 Buchanan: feeling thermometer (362)

On a scale of 0 to 100 degrees, how warm or cool do you feel toward Pat Buchanan? (assessed before the election)

V211 Lieberman: feeling thermometer (366)

On a scale of 0 to 100 degrees, how warm or cool do you feel toward Joseph Kieberman? (assessed before the election)

V212 Cheney: feeling thermometer (367)

On a scale of 0 to 100 degrees, how warm or cool do you feel toward Richard Cheney? (assessed before the election)

V213 Clinton: feeling thermometer (359)

On a scale of 0 to 100 degrees, how warm or cool do you feel toward Bill Clinton? (assessed before the election)

V214 Democratic Party: feeling thermometer (369)

On a scale of 0 to 100 degrees, how warm or cool do you feel toward the Democratic Party? (assessed before the election)

V215 Republican Party: feeling thermometer (370)

On a scale of 0 to 100 degrees, how warm or cool do you feel toward the Republican Party? (assessed before the election)

V216 Political parties: feeling thermometer

On a scale of 0 to 100 degrees, how warm or cool do you feel toward political parties in general? (assessed before the election)

V217 Congress: feeling thermometer (1305)

On a scale of 0 to 100 degrees, how warm or cool do you feel toward Congress? (assessed after the election)

V218 Conservatives: feeling thermometer (1310)

On a scale of 0 to 100 degrees, how warm or cool do you feel toward conservatives? (assessed after the election)

V219 Liberals: feeling thermometer (1311)

On a scale of 0 to 100 degrees, how warm or cool do you feel toward liberals? (assessed after the election)

V220: Labor unions: feeling thermometer (1312)

On a scale of 0 to 100 degrees, how warm or cool do you feel toward labor unions? (assessed after the election)

V221: Big business: feeling thermometer (1313)

On a scale of 0 to 100 degrees, how warm or cool do you feel toward big business? (assessed after the election)

V222: Age (908)

Respondent's age.

References

Abramson, Paul R., John H. Aldrich, and David W. Rhode. 1999. *Continuity and Change in the 1996 and 1998 Elections*. Washington: CQ Press.

Balz, Dan, and Richard Morin. 2000. The Voters Grade Bush and Gore. *Washington Post National Weekly Edition*, 10 July, 6.

Barstow, David. 2000. Gore, Invoking Image of 'Silent Spring' Author, Talks of Defending Environment. *New York Times*. 13 August, A19.

Barstow, David, and Don Van Natta, Jr. 2001. How Bush Took Florida: Mining the Overseas Absentee Vote. *New York Times*, 15 July, A1.

Berelson, Bernard R., Paul F. Lazarsfeld, and William N. McPhee. 1954. *Voting*. Chicago: University of Chicago Press.

Black, Earl, and Merle Black. 1992. *The Vital South*. Cambridge, MA: Harvard University Press.

Burnham, Walter Dean. 1970. *Critical Elections and the Mainspring of American Politics*. New York: W.W. Norton.

Campbell, Angus, Philip E. Converse, Warren E. Miller, and Donald E. Stokes. 1960. *The American Voter*. New York: John Wiley.

Campbell, James E. 2000. *The American Campaign*. College Station, TX: Texas A&M University Press.

Campbell, James E. 2001. The Referendum That Didn't Happen: The Forecasts of the 2000 Presidential Election. *PS: Political Science and Politics* 34 (March), 33-38.

Ceasar, James W., and Andrew E. Busch. 2001. *The Perfect Tie*. Lanham, MD: Rowman and Littlefield.

Clymer, Adam. 2000. Surplus a Gulf Between Candidates. *New York Times*, 30 April, A22.

Converse, Philip E. 1964. The Nature of Belief Systems in Mass Publics. In *Ideology and Discontent*, edited by David E. Apter. New York: The Free Press.

Converse, Philip E. 1970. Attitudes and Nonattitudes: The Continuation of a Dialogue. In *The Quantitative Analysis of Social Problems*, edited by Edward Tufte. Reading, MA: Addison-Wesley.

Converse, Philip E., and Gregory B. Markus. 1979. Plus ca Change ...: The New CPS Election Study Panel. *American Political Science Review* 73 (March), 32-49.

Corrado, Anthony. 2001. Financing the 2000 Elections. In *The Election of 2000: Reports and Interpretations*, edited by Gerald M. Pomper. New York: Chatham House Publishers of Seven Bridges Press.

Crotty, William. 2001. The Presidential Primaries: Triumph of the Frontrunners. In *America's Choices*, edited by William Crotty. Boulder, CO: Westview Press.

Elder, Janet. 2000. Four New Polls Show Bush With an Edge, and Nader a Factor. *New York Times*, 7 November, A19.

Erikson, Robert S., and Karl Sigman. 2000. Gore Favored in the Electoral College. Paper posted at: www.ieor.columbia.edu/~sigman, 5 November.

Erickson, Robert S., and Kent Tedin. 1995. *American Public Opinion*, 5th ed. Boston: Allyn and Bacon.

Frankovic, Kathleen, and Monika L. McDermott. 2001. Public Opinion in the 2000 Election: The Ambivalent Electorate. In *The Election of 2000: Reports and Interpretations*, edited by Gerald M. Pomper. New York: Chatham House Publishers of Seven Bridges Press.

Fiorina, Morris P. 1981. *Retrospective Voting in American National Elections*. New Haven, CT: Yale University Press.

Herrnson, Paul S. 2001. The Congressional Elections. In *The Election of 2000: Reports and Interpretations*, edited by Gerald M. Pomper. New York: Chatham House Publishers of Seven Bridges Press.

Gallup Organization. 1996. Clinton, Dole, Gingrich: Handling of Budget Negotiations. *The Gallup Poll Monthly*, January, 14-38.

Gallup Organization. 1998. Public Leans Against Impeachment Hearings; Holds Fast Against Removal From Office. Poll Analyses, 10 October. Accessed at: www.gallup.com/poll/releases/pr981010.

Gallup Organization. 1999. Public Sends Mixed Signals About Bill Clinton. Poll Analyses, 9 April. Accessed at: www.gallup.com/poll/releases/pr990409.

Gallup Organization. 2000a. Clinton Job Approval Remains Steady at 58%. Poll Analyses, 11 October. Accessed at: www.gallup.com/poll/releases/pr001011c.

Gallup Organization. 2000b. Debates Net Positive For Bush. Poll Analyses, 21 October. Accessed at: www.gallup.com/poll/releases/pr001021.

Gallup Organization. 2000c. Major Turning Points in 2000 Election: Primary Season, Conventions, and Debates. Poll Releases, 7 November. Accessed at: www.gallup.com/poll/releases/pr001107.

Jacobson, Gary C. 2001. Congress: Elections and Stalemate. In *The Elections of 2000*, edited by Michael Nelson. Washington, DC: CQ Press.

Katosh, John P., and Michael W. Traugott. 1981. The Consequences of Vali dated and Self-reported Voting Measures. *Public Opinion Quarterly* 45: 519-35.

Kelley, Stanley, Jr. 1983. *Interpreting Elections*. Princeton, NJ: Princeton University Press.

Kiewiet, D. Roderick. 1983. *Macroeconomics and Micropolitics*. Chicago: University of Chicago Press.

Ladd, Everett Carll, Jr., and Charles D. Hadley. 1978. *Transformations of the American Party System*, 2nd ed. New York: Norton, 1978.

Mayer, William G. 2001. The Presidential Nominations. In *The Election of 2000: Reports and Interpretations*, edited by Gerald M. Pomper. New York: Chatham House Publishers of Seven Bridges Press.

Miller, Warren E., and J. Merrill Shanks. 1996. *The New American Voter*. Cambridge, MA: Harvard University Press.

Mitchell, Alison. 2000. After Attacks, Bush Strikes Back Hard in Defense of His Social Security Proposal. *New York Times*, 20 October, A21.

Mueller, Carol M., ed. 1988. *The Politics of the Gender Gap*. Newbury Park, CA: Sage Publications.

Nelson, Michael. 2001. The Election: Ordinary Politics, Extraordinary Outcome. In *The Elections of 2000*, edited by Michael Nelson. Washington, DC: CQ

Press.

Nie, Norman H., Sidney Verba, and John R. Petrocik. 1976. *The Changing American Voter.* Cambridge, MA: Harvard University Press.

Page, Benjamin I. 1978. *Choices and Echoes in Presidential Elections.* Chicago: University of Chicago Press.

Popkin, Samuel L. 1991. *The Reasoning Voter.* Chicago: The University of Chicago Press.

Shapiro, Robert Y., and Harpeet Mahajan. 1986. Gender Difference in Public Preferences: A Summary of Trends From the 1960s to the 1980s. *Public Opinion Quarterly* 50 (Spring): 47-55.

Seltzer, Richard A., Jody Newman, and Melissa Voorhees Leighton. 1997. Sex as a Political Variable. Boulder, CO: Lynne Rienner.

Stanley, Harold W. 2001. The Nominations: The Return of the Party Leaders. In *The Elections of 2000*, edited by Michael Nelson. Washington, DC: CQ Press.

Stouffer, Samuel A. 1955. *Communism, Conformity and Civil Liberties.* New York: Doubleday.

Sundquist, James L. 1983. *The Dynamics of the Party System*, rev. ed. Washington: The Brookings Institution.

Toner, Robin. 2000a. Reissue of Gore Book May Be a Two-edged Sword. *New York Times*, 14 April, A21.

Toner, Robin. 2000b. Gore and Bush Health Proposals Fall Short of Counter parts' Plans 8 Years Ago. *New York Times*, 15 October, A22.

Traugott, Michael W., and Paul J. Lavrakas. 2000. The Voter's Guide to Election Polls, 2nd ed. New York: Chatham House Publishers of Seven Bridges Press.

Van Natta, Don, Jr. 1999. Polling's Dirty Little Secret: No Response (Most People Approached by Pollsters Refuse to Cooperate). *New York Times*, 21 November, 1.

Voter.com. 2000. National and State Polls on the Presidential Race. Voter.com, 5 November. Accessed at: www.voter.com.

Wald, Kenneth D. 1987. *Religion and Politics in the United States.* New York: St. Martin's Press.

Wattenberg, Martin P. 1994. *The Decline of American Political Parties, 1952-1992.* Cambridge, MA: Harvard University Press.

Weisberg, Herbert F., Jon A. Krosnick, and Bruce D. Bowen. 1996. *An Introduction to Survey Research and Data Analysis*, 3rd ed. Glenview, IL: Scott, Foresman, and Company.

APPENDIX
TECHNICAL NOTE TO THE INSTRUCTOR

The data for this SETUPS are drawn from the 2000 American National Election Study (ANES) Pre- and Post-Election Survey. These data were collected by the Center for Political Studies (CPS) and are distributed by the Inter-University Consortium for Political and Social Research (ICPSR). The principle investigators for the 2000 ANES were Nancy Burns, Donald R. Kinder, Steven J. Rosenstone, and Virginia Sapiro. Further information on the 2000 ANES can be obtained from the ICPSR home page (http://www.icpsr.umich.edu).

Only the 1555 respondents who were interviewed both before and after the election are included in this dataset. A total of 160 categoric variables (V001 to V160) have been drawn, or in some cases created, from the data in the full ANES file (ICPSR study number 3131). Most of the variables have been recoded to simplify matters for the students by reducing the number of response categories, and in many cases a single variable has been created to combine a filter screen with its corresponding question. In other cases, several variables have been combined into a single index. The SETUPS codebook gives the original reference number (or numbers if more than one original variable was used) for each variable, so that you can refer to the full ANES codebook to obtain information on the original coding or the exact wording of each item.

In addition to the 160 categoric variables, 22 interval-level variables have been included (see variables V201 to V222). These variables may be useful to instructors who want their students to use statistical techniques, such as regression analysis, that are less appropriate for categoric data. While we anticipate that most instructors will use only the categoric variables and crosstabulation analyses, as these are more appropriate for most undergraduates, some instructors, especially those using these materials in research methods courses, may welcome the ability to use the data for more advanced statistical methods.

The design of the 2000 ANES is complex. Some of the respondents were interviewed in person before and after the election. Others received telephone interviews. Some were interviewed in person before the election but by telephone afterward. Because of differences in the response rates for different interview groups, the unequal probability of selection of respondents in different size households, and the under-representation or over-representation of certain demographic groups in the sample, the data should be weighted for any analysis. The appropriate weight (ANES variable V000002a, post-weight) is included in the dataset (as WEIGHT) but is not listed in the codebook. The weighting of the data generally will be transparent to the student users. It might be noted, however, that while 1555 respondents completed the post-election interview, the weighted data produce a total of 1554 respondents.

The dataset for this SETUPS is available from the ICPSR as study 3356. The data may be obtained from the ICPSR on diskette or downloaded from the ICPSR Internet site. Faculty at ICPSR member institutions automatically have the right to access to these data; they should contact their ICPSR Official Representative (OR) to place an order through the ICPSR's CDNet or to download the data from the ICPSR Internet site. Faculty at nonmember institutions will be eligible to receive the data upon ordering the SETUPS monographs for class adoption. When an order for the monographs is placed with the APSA, the faculty member will receive an order form and ordering instructions for the dataset. The data normally will be sent on diskette to faculty at nonmember institutions; alternative arrangements may discussed with the ICPSR.

This SETUPS is prepared especially for SPSS users, but those who prefer to use a different statistical package should be accommodated. In some cases, the SPSS file can be directly imported into the other statistical package; in other cases, a raw data file can be written out from the SPSS file, and the raw data file can be imported into the other package. The data file that is distributed is an SPSS portable file.

The SPSS file contains a full set of variable and value labels. These labels are identified in the codebook. There are two variables in the dataset that are not described in the codebook: CASENUM (the respondent's interview identification number) and WEIGHT (the weight factor). The case number is not necessary for the use of these data, but it would be essential if a user wanted to pull additional variables from the full ANES and merge them with these data, and we have included it to allow for that possibility. The WEIGHT variable should be included and any analysis should use the weighted data, as discussed above. Please note that if you create an SPSS file from the portable file provided, you will need to turn on the weight factor.

Contact Us

We welcome comments and reactions, positive or negative, from users of this instructional package. This information may be of great use in subsequent editions. Please send your feedback to either coauthor:

Charles Prysby, *Department of Political Science, University of North Carolina at Greensboro, Greensboro, NC 27402-6170. Email: prysby@uncg.edu.*

Carmine Scavo, *Department of Political Science, East Carolina University, Greenville, NC 27858-4353. Email: scavoc@mail.ecu.edu.*

Notes

Notes

Supplemental **E**mpirical **T**eaching **U**nits in **P**olitical **S**cience

Titles available in the SETUPS in American Politics Series

Voting Behavior: The 2000 Election
by Charles Prysby and Carmine Scavo

Voting Behavior: The 1996 Election
by Charles Prysby and Carmine Scavo

American Voting Behavior in Presidential Elections from 1972 to 1992
by Charles Prysby and Carmine Scavo

Voting Behavior: The 1992 Election
by Charles Prysby and Carmine Scavo

How to Order

Manuals (containing the codebook) may be ordered from the American Political Science Association: 1). online through APSA's publications catalogue and secure server at **www.apsanet.org/pubs,** or 2).by telephone at **202-483-2512** (APSA Publications).

Datasets are available from the Inter-University Consortium for Political and Social Research (ICPSR) to faculty and students who have purchased the guidebook. Institutional members of ICPSR may request the data directly from ICPSR. Non-ICPSR departments will receive a data order form from APSA with their shipments of SETUPS manuals.

Are Your Students Wondering What Career Paths are Available to Them?

Cartoon by Ted Mann, courtesy of the *Williams Record*

Careers and the Study of Political Science: A Guide for Undergraduates

Sixth Edition (2001)

Exploring a variety of careers, this updated career book offers students a host of advice and references (print and online) to aid them in their career search. This book will guide students in:

- *Analysing skills and interests, especially those developed through the study of political science*
- *Discovering the personal and civic value in studying political science,*
- *Exploring a variety of career paths available to them:*
  - *Federal, state and local government,*
  - *Nonprofits and nongovernmental organizations,*
  - *Law, business,*
  - *International careers,*
  - *Journalism,*
  - *Campaigns and polling,*
  - *Precollegiate education,*
  - *M.A. and Ph.D. careers, and*
  - *Public Service*
- *Choosing a career*

APSA Publications

Order APSA publications online at www.apsanet.org/pubs or call APSA Publications at 202-483-2512.

Career Video!

Career Encounters : Political Science

A perfect companion to *Careers and the Study of Political Science*

This 28 ½ minute career video, produced by the American Political Science Association, features conversations with ten people with meaningful and rewarding careers who studied political science in college. Their stories convey the many career opportunities and personal rewards associated with taking undergraduate classes in political science, public policy and international relations to students at all levels of education and all types of institutions: high schools, two-year colleges, and four-year colleges and universities.

The careers featured on the film are:

*   Secretary, Department of Health and Human Services, The Clinton Administration
*   Legislative Director, for Dennis Hastert (R-IL), Speaker of the House, 106th Congress
*   Professor, Haverford College
*   Project Director, Rock the Vote
*   Attorney
*   Market Researcher
*   President, Montgomery County School Board, & Lobbyist, National School Boards Association
*   Director of Development, Greater Chicago Food Depository
*   High School Government Teacher
*   News Anchor

The viewer's guide, excerpts of the interviews and additional information about the video are available online at **www.apsanet.org/pubs/careervideo.cfm**.

The *Career Encounters*® career exploration series is produced by Davis Gray, Inc.

Considering undergraduate study in political science?

Political Science: An Ideal Liberal Arts Major

A brochure about the skills and career opportunities acquired through a political science major.

Political science majors hone writing, communication, analytical and computer skills that are critical to a liberal arts education. This kind of education will prepare students to think critically and independently. Majoring in political science will open doors for you to many different careers in public sector organizations (business, law, consulting, state, local and federal government, journalism, political campaigns and polling, interest groups, etc) as well as private for- and non-profit organizations.

This brochure gives students considering the political science major advice about how to pursue the major and about the career possibilities available to them.

Considering graduate study in political science?

Earning a Ph.D. in Political Science

A brochure with advice on why and how to pursue graduate study in political science.

This guide provides answers about:
- *Qualifications necessary for graduate study,*
- *Selecting a graduate program,*
- *Financial aid,*
- *Timetable to apply to graduate school,*
- *What occurs in graduate school, and*
- *Careers available to political science Ph.D.s inside and outside academe.*

APSA Publications

Order these publications online at www.apsanet.org/pubs or call APSA Publications at 202-483-2512.